SEAL ≈ Test

SEAL ≈ Test

a novel

by George Vercessi

ISBN:978-1-5850-0310-5 (sf)

ISBN: 978-1-4520-1665-8 (e)

This book is printed on acid free paper.

1stBooks –rev. 4/29/2010

Disclaimer

The characters and events depicted in this story are entirely fictional. Any resemblance to actual persons, living or dead, is purely coincidental.

Prologue

(Tehran, Iran)

Memorandum for Our Great Spiritual Leader
Subject: The Confluence of Circumstances

Like the great planets in the universe, during those rare instances when their orbits bring them into perfect alignment setting monumental events in motion that cannot be stopped or altered, we have arrived at a similar juncture. Circumstances are such that we can now successfully advance the cause of Mohammed in a manner that will ensure domination over the diseased infidels.

The first element of consideration. Our eternal enemy, The Great Satan, has unilaterally disarmed himself to the point where he no longer has the means or the will to interfere in our Holy crusade. U. S. defense spending is at a fifty year low, less than three percent of its gross national product! The force structure of his once powerful military has been reduced by half of what it was during the Persian Gulf War. He has withdrawn most of his forward deployed forces back to his distant shores, leaving only token forces in their stead. Unquestionably, he is no longer capable of mounting the same large-scale force as quickly as he did in 1991 against our eternal foe, Iraq. Attempting such a monumental task now would claim more young American lives than he is prepared to expend while costing his shrinking economy dearly. Underscoring this point, the American Under Secretary of State publicly summed up his administration's policy when he said, "The U. S. doesn't have the influence, inclination or the money to use military forces as they had in the past." Nor, can America any longer turn to its allies for support. Its foolish bungling in the foreign policy arena has exhausted their cache of international esteem.

Second. By committing most of his key air and sealift assets to that ludicrous body politic, the UN, our enemy has further diminished his war fighting capacity.

Third. Morale within his armed forces has reached record lows. Enlistments and retentions are dangerously low. Meanwhile, his military leaders helplessly watch their commander-in-chief, through ineptitude or calculation, dismantle and weaken them. Unlike our northern Turkish neighbors, whose generals have been forced to wrest control from feeble presidents, the evil Americans can be counted on to do nothing.

Fourth. Americans, to their credit, have overcome many diseases but they have failed miserably to tackle one malady about which, we fortunately know little. The Great Satan, President Pickens, like many of his fellow citizens, is the by-product of that unique western sin, alcoholism.

He is a paradigm of hyperactivity - he overeats, overworks and prefers travelling to remaining in the Oval Office. To date, he has spent more time away from the White House than any of his predecessors. Further, like all dysfunctionals, he lives in a fantasy world, in which he denies truth and reality, particularly when under pressure. In sum, he is weak of character and easily capable of being manipulated simply by creating dissonance in his well-ordered world.

Given the above, it is urged that we implement our plan immediately!

YOUR COMMENTS: *Let us begin.*

* * *

(Washington, DC)

Memorandum For the President
Subject: Iranian Military Buildup

DoD and CIA have recently completed their annual analysis of the Persian Gulf states Order of Battle. Of particular concern is the manner in which Iran has increased its military strength in the face of a diminishing threat from its longtime enemy to the west. CIA believes Tehran is taking advantage of the turmoil brought on by the United Nations embargo against Iraq and the prospect that civil war may soon erupt there. While Saddam Hussein struggles to maintain power under the weight of a crumbling economy, his energies are being sapped by militant Kurds in the north and rebels in the south. Thus weakened, Iran has moved steadily forward, amassing arms to the point where it now poses a significant threat not only to Iraq but to all of its gulf neighbors.

Secretary of Defense Gartland and CIA Director Hemmings are prepared to brief you on Iran's growing military forces, augmented recently by two Russian Kilo class submarines, a new fleet of attack patrol boats, armed with Chinese anti-ship Styx missiles to replace the inaccurate and unreliable Silkworms, and North Korean Scud-B and Scud-C missiles. Further, Iran has funded North Korea's Nodong missile program. [For your information, Mr. President, the Nodong-1 has a range of 600 miles, which makes it capable of striking any of the gulf states, while the Nodong-2, constructed with lighter materials, has an extended 200 mile range, which puts Israel in Iran's target range.] Of equal concern is that Iran may be using its nuclear reactor project in Bushehr as a cover for acquiring sensitive Russian technology.

Additional background.

- Japan has already informed Iran that purchasing the Nodong would be the equivalent of crossing a diplomatic red line, forcing Tokyo to sever relations with Tehran.
- Using diplomatic channels, we are urging our allies to apply similar pressure on North Korea to cease selling missiles in the Middle East.

YOUR COMMENTS: *Very interesting. I understand the problem. I'll skip the briefing.*

ACTION: *None required. Thank you, LP*

D Minus Eleven
(Annapolis, Maryland)

Chapter One

Despite their professor's determination to inject enthusiasm into his lecture on the *feedback effects of nuclear reactor kinetics*, the heavy lunch and prospects of the long Thanksgiving weekend just hours away conspired against the most studious midshipmen. With the lecturer's droning voice growing dimmer in his sphere of consciousness, Midshipman firstclass Russell Bennett, II, fidgeted in the last row, where he sat believing it would save him from being called upon by the bespectacled professor. Like most of his classmates, Bennett's attention was everywhere but where it should be in this, his final class of the day. Knowing the session would go right to the hour wasn't helping matters, either.

Dr. Charlie Nolan had been at the Naval Academy for decades and his dedication to turning out the best officers in the fleet was legendary. It would never occur to him to cut his lecture by so much as a minute despite the tendency of more liberal colleagues to do so on these holiday eves. Long before being selected chairman of the Naval Systems Engineering Division he had made a commitment to those specially selected students pursuing a career in the Navy's complex nuclear propulsion program, even if sometimes they lacked the same commitment. It was a task he relished and in which he took great pride, as evidenced by the list of distinguished former students he distributed along with the course outline on the first day of every new class. Arranged by rank, it was a *Who's Who* of alumni who had risen to command the fleet and in several instances, gone on to command the Navy.

On this holiday eve, a Navy career was the farthest thing on Bennett's mind. Instead, he was lusting after Ingrid Lucerne, his nubile, straight-A classmate, who was seated below him in the front row of the small amphitheater. In fact, it could be said with certainty, that she was frequently in his thoughts. With his

1

hormones pumping, he raised his pen and began tracing an imaginary line around her profile. Starting from her forehead, he inched around her strong, sculptured chin and down her neck, while thinking how he'd replicate the journey with his tongue once they were alone together. He was focusing the pen point and his thoughts on the tips of her breasts which, contrary to academy regs, he'd fondled in hideaways around the yard since classes had begun in September and which to his delight, were now straining the buttons of her tailored shirt, when she turned and caught him. Offering a wink and a cheshire smile, she arched her back and pushed out her breasts in a way that indicated she knew what he was thinking. Further aroused, he shifted anxiously in his seat amid a chorus of throat clearings from several envious classmates.

Unaware of the cause, and without breaking his stride, Nolan simply raised an eyebrow to re-establish order. Meanwhile, a shadowy figure in the hall stopped and peered through the small window in the center of the door then moved on. It was a minor, but frequent occurrence that went largely unnoticed among those so accustomed to living in a fish bowl. Only Bancroft Hall, the massive dormitory, was off limits to everyone but company officers. Outside the dorm, life at the academy was one long series of exhibitions - academic and athletic alike - and all were ruled by the tight schedule contained in the official *Plan of the Day*. With so many activities squeezed into each day there was little tolerance for interruptions, particularly during the precious fifty-minute lectures. Not even the superintendent, a two-star admiral, would intrude without first alerting the department head, who then checked with the division chairman, and so on down the line. And, since the tenured faculty guarded their domain with the tenacity of pit bulls, one could correctly assume such disruptions were infrequent.

So, when the door swung open and five men in business suits walked in, Professor Nolan reacted predictably by looking up in mid-sentence and demanding an explanation.

"I beg your pardon, gentlemen. As you can see, there's a class in progress. What's the meaning of this?" He was a small, thin man but his tone conveyed the full authority of his senior faculty rank.

Ignoring his protestations, four of the intruders moved with military swiftness along the wall to the rear of the room. The fifth one, a massive and odious looking man, closed the door and wedged his heel firmly against it while pressing his huge frame against the small window. Happy for any diversion, the mids watched in fascination as Nolan, scowling, crossed the room to challenge the stranger.

"Sorry for the disruption, Professor Nolan," he said. Though his words and demeanor were courteous, his menacing looks and peculiar air of command made Nolan falter at the sound of his name. "We're here at the request of the superintendent, Rear Admiral Harding," he explained in a flat, even tone, implying this interruption should be considered routine.

But Nolan wasn't having any of it and he shook his head and waved a disapproving finger. "I don't care who sent you. This is *my* class and you don't belong here."

To the mids' amusement, the bearded stranger countered by producing a wallet which he flipped open and held at arm's length, revealing a gold badge and photo ID.

"This is an anti-terrorist drill, professor," he announced, as if that were sufficient explanation.

"Why haven't I been alerted?" Nolan argued. Then, resolving to take it up with the Academic Dean, he said, a bit petulantly, "There are procedures, you know."

The stranger seemed not to care. Exhaling, he shook his head and everyone knew he'd heard similar protestations before.

"Professor," he sighed, "this is an *anti-terrorist exercise*." The words came off his tongue slowly but malevolently, like the hissing of a snake. "We conduct them at installations around the world. Part of our effectiveness, as the admiral well knows, is coming into a facility without prior warning. Just, as you might expect," he stressed with a crooked smile, "the *real* bad guys would do. Now, my men and I are here to simulate a hostage takeover. The supe was emphatic that we use this class as the target. I don't know why," he said, allowing a hint of irritation to

3

emerge. "And, you know what, professor? I frankly don't give a damn. Only his immediate staff knew we were coming."

"But, we've never done anything like this before." Nolan appeared less angry and more resigned, now.

"Precisely, professor. That's what this is all about. The school has a contingency crisis plan that's never been activated. The admiral wants it tested. The best way to test it is with a realistic simulation. You don't achieve realism by being notified in advance. Besides," he said with obvious impatience, "if you'd been consulted, I can assure you others around the yard would've learned of it and the element of surprise - a critical ingredient in the real world - would've been lost." He was becoming anxious and, checking his watch, he added brusquely, "And, if we don't hustle this whole exercise'll have been a waste of time. So, kindly give us your full cooperation. If you got problems, I suggest you take them up with the admiral at the post-exercise briefing. For now, I'm running the show and we're running out of time. For your safety, I urge you to do as I say."

Nolan was about to speak but jumped back when the man produced a gun from his waistband, the tip wrapped with red day-glo tape.

"This," he announced to the owl-eyed professor and rapt students, "is a prop. It's real," he assured them, "but we use red tape to denote that it isn't loaded. As you'll see, we strive for realism throughout the exercise," he explained to the class rather than the ashen-faced professor. "I assure you this will be a great learning experience for all of you." Then, checking his watch again, he announced, "All right. We're approaching the hour and we need to move quickly, before classes change. I want you to stay close together as we leave the building. There's a van waiting that my men will escort you to. Once inside, we'll drive directly to the field house, where we've arranged to take over one of the visiting team's locker rooms. From there, we'll simulate a hostage negotiation scenario. Please don't shout, scream or do anything to attract attention. They'll be plenty of time for that later. The object, now, is to get you out of the building with minimum disruption. If this were the real thing the bad guys would gag and cuff you. But," he said with a conspiratorial grin, "that won't be necessary today. The point of this phase of the exercise is to test the school's ability to respond in an effective and timely manner. Any questions?"

The mids, pleased for the disruption, shook their heads as the leader holstered his gun and buttoned his jacket. Then, opening the door slightly, he checked the hallway. Satisfied, he turned and said, much as a coach to his waiting team, "Okay. Grab your belongings and go!"

He held the door as the ten mids, under the watchful eyes of their escorts, cheerfully ran for the van while Nolan looked on helplessly.

Then, raising his eyebrows and shrugging his resignation, he collected his notes and moved to join his students, saying, "Well, I guess such precautions were inevitable. The world has really gone to pieces."

The man's powerful arm across Nolan's chest prevented him from going any farther.

* * *

"I've never seen this before," the Junior Officer of the Day commented, while completing the tally of muster reports gathered from the evening meal formation.

"Never seen what before?" replied the Midshipman Officer of the Day from his desk across the room.

"So many absentees over and above those excused for medical reasons, sir." He walked over and placed the list on his superior's desk, murmuring, "And, most of them firstclassmen. I guess they departed early for Thanksgiving."

"That's not surprising," the senior said as he scanned the names. "You know what they say. RHIP."

The comment drew a vacant look.

"Rank has its privileges," the senior mid explained impatiently.

"Whatdya mean?" he asked, studying the list again.

"Bennett! Lucerne! Valerius! Zablocki!" came the response.

There was a long silence.

"Still don't get it, do you?"

"No, sir."

"I don't remember being this dumb as a plebe," the other mid groused. Then with parental patience, he went down the list. "Bennett. His father's Senator Bennett, Chairman of the Foreign Relations Committee. Lucerne. Her daddy's Marine Corps General John Lucerne, Vice Chairman, and currently acting Chairman of the Joint Chiefs of Staff."

He paused, allowing his charge to grasp it.

"What about the others? Who're their fathers?"

"I don't know. Probably nobody. But, Valerius is one of the best cross country athletes in years and that's enough to get him special treatment."

"And the other one? Zablocki?"

"You've got a lot to learn, mister. How'd you spend plebe summer? Jerking off under the sheets? Next year he'll be a Rhodes Scholar. One of the brainiest guys around. He's won more honors than anyone around here can remember. He'll be number one academically at graduation."

"Impressive. I guess they're entitled to skip evening meal formation," he offered while the other mid leafed through a second folder on his desk.

"Hmmm. Not so fast," the senior replied after comparing the absentees with those authorized early holiday departure by the commandant.

"But, you just said...,"

"Forget what I said. Ten of the fourteen are absent without leave!" He noted the time - it was six-fifteen - then picked up the phone and dialed the commandant's office.

*   *   *

Meanwhile, across the quadrangle, Lieutenant Tom Fitzgerald began the ritual of securing Rickover Hall for the night. As duty officer for the Engineering Department, he was responsible for ensuring all windows were closed and locked, classroom lights were off and, excepting faculty, that the building was empty. Starting on the top floor he worked his way methodically along the empty corridors down to the ground floor. It was a mindless, housekeeping task and he hummed casually as he went along. His thoughts were focused on the pandemonium awaiting him at home, where his family and visiting relatives were putting the final touches on the big Thanksgiving dinner tomorrow. It was to be one of the few holidays in his ten year career that he wasn't at sea and he was eager to get home and begin it.

At six-thirty he completed his rounds and returned to his office, where he signed the duty log, grabbed his brief case and headed for the exit. On the way, he stopped at the water fountain and as he stepped away he noticed a thick, dark liquid oozing out from under the adjoining janitor's closet. Curious, he opened the door and flicked on the light then stumbled backwards. Stuffed in the corner, behind several mops and buckets, his head angled awkwardly against the wall, was Professor Nolan. His eyes were open and staring blankly back at him. His throat was slit and blood seeped from the grisly wound onto the floor.

Chapter Two

Humming to the low strain of holiday tunes being piped into his expansive office, Ambassador Jennings Arnold was more focused on the Thanksgiving dinner that afternoon than the morning cables he was scanning, the bulk of which he had already determined could wait until the following day. Reading the high volume of traffic was an essential and unavoidable part of his daily routine. It was usually the first order of business and a chore he'd grown to disdain along with the demanding, round-the-clock State Department work ethic. If he could have avoided it today, he would have done so, gladly. After all, it was a holiday back home and that, he reasoned, made it one at the embassy, too. And, since there were no pressing issues on his agenda, why then shouldn't he and his American staff enjoy it.

The cables, stacked neatly on his desk when he had arrived, were in varying colored folders denoting their priority; among them, red being the highest. Having been culled by the duty officer from the hundreds of messages received the previous night, they represented a fraction of the embassy's high volume of traffic. Carefully screened and highlighted, they had been inserted into the appropriate folders in order of importance, a routine procedure in every embassy and one that worked best where inexperienced political appointees like Arnold reigned. And, while he disliked the task, he appreciated the system that effectively aided him in grasping the nuances of international communiques as well as the knottier, more complex issues. Today, among the messages he shunted aside was the *Weekly Terrorist Intelligence Summary*, a lengthy and tedious report which he'd learned early on didn't offer much in the way of timely or pertinent intelligence. It was the same criticism shared by career foreign service officers, who had ceased relying on it soon after the current administration slashed the intel community's budget. Now, the best the sterile report had to offer was a summary of hot spots, listed alphabetically by region. Usually, one could do as well, if not better, with CNN. There were exceptions, of course. Such as the 1993 New York World Trade Center bombing, when the FBI provided some real intelligence analysis that never made the evening news, but they were rare. Consequently, Arnold used it as his fellow diplomats did; as a headline service from which to draw items of interest on Egypt and the surrounding region. Then, if he wished, he could pursue a specific issue via back channel communications with any number of government agencies.

On this day, the lead report in the summary touched on the murder of a U. S. Naval Academy professor then segued into an ambiguous assessment that the death might be terrorist-related. No mention was made of the disappearance or whereabouts of the missing midshipmen. The Chief of Naval Operations had persuaded the Secretary of Defense to omit that aspect of the tragedy from the report until more was known.

Arnold completed reading the last folder and placed it squarely in the center of his polished walnut OUT box but not before removing the President's and the Secretary of State's Thanksgiving Day messages to all foreign service employees abroad. Folding each precisely, he slipped them into an envelope, which he then placed inside his coat pocket. Later, he would extract the greetings at the staff luncheon, reading each as if it was a personal missive sent directly to him by grateful colleagues. Patting his jacket, the portly diplomat surveyed his large desk and straightened items that didn't need straightening. He then rose and strolled to the window overlooking the walled compound and the hectic city beyond. The day was gray and cool, as it might be back in Indiana. Recollections of home and of his lifetime accomplishments brought a smile. Imagine! he mused, smugly. Jennings Arnold... *the Honorable* Jennings Arnold... *Mr. Ambassador*. It was the culmination of a long and profitable career. And it mattered little that as a businessman, he lacked experience in the high stakes game of international diplomacy. He'd paid his dues in the form of extraordinary contributions to

10

President Pickens' campaign. That was ample justification. Henceforth, wherever he went, he'd carry the title of Ambassador. He looked at his watch. It was eleven-thirty. Everyone would be downstairs at the reception. It was time to make his entrance. Turning from the window, he paused at his desk to align the marble base of his gold pen and pencil set with the Moroccan leather diary beside it. He also brushed away a speck of dust which only his meticulous eye would see. Satisfied, he moved to the mirror by the door, checked his tie and handkerchief and left.

Downstairs, Arnold mingled contentedly with his staff, bestowing holiday wishes like blessings. Playing god was what he liked doing most. And, as ambassador, he was pretty close to being one. He was circling the room, a drink in hand, dispensing bon mots when his assistant interrupted and whispered they needed to speak privately.

"What's the problem, Saunders? Has World War III started without my permission?" he said with a careless laugh.

John Saunders, who had a dry sense of humor and took his job a little too seriously, failed to respond in kind.

Noting his career officer's anxious look, Arnold shrugged and set his wine glass and plate of hors d'oeuvres on a nearby table before following the older man out to the hallway. As he exited, he smiled at staff members who were happy for his attention.

"Nothing so drastic, sir," his second-in-command whispered as they walked.

Saunders specialized in middle eastern affairs. He'd arrived in Cairo two weeks before Arnold with the standard State Department instructions to oversee the operations while keeping his boss from making a fool of himself and embarrassing the United States.

"Good. I'd hate to disrupt our little party. It's not often we get to socialize with the worker bees."

Arnold's unearned snobbery had offended Saunders, a true Boston Brahmin, since their first days together.

"What's the problem then?"

11

"We've received a package marked urgent and for your eyes only. But, what bothers me most is that it's from the Swiss and we weren't expecting anything from them."

"Well maybe it's fondue for our party," he said with more of a laugh than Saunders thought the witless comment justified.

"Seriously, sir. The Swiss are very predictable. They would never send something without first advising us. Nevertheless, it was delivered by diplomatic courier and it does bear their markings. I think you should examine it."

"Must I do so now? Can't we at least wait until after the meal? I'm starving," he whined.

"I've had it brought to your office. It should only take a moment and I'm sure you'll be back in time for the ceremonial cutting of the turkey," he said with a reassuring smile. "Besides, the Swiss may be waiting for a response."

"Alright, then."

The neatly wrapped package, about eight inches square, was waiting for him in the center of his desk.

"Yep. You're right, John. It sure seems to be from our Swiss friends. Did you have it run through the bomb detection as a precaution?" he said, while moving behind the desk.

"Of course, sir."

Arnold picked it up and shook it.

"Careful, sir. It might be breakable."

"Well, it's not my birthday. What the hell could it be? Maybe it's an early Christmas present."

"There's one way to find out, sir." Saunders was losing his patience.

"Right. Let's get on with it and get back downstairs."

He tore off the wrapping, revealing a handsome inlaid cedar box, its cover held in place by an intricate brass hasp.

"If the contents are half as nice as the package, it's sure to be spectacular," he said.

Saunders watched him fumble with the latch then remove a smaller, styrofoam container that was taped shut.

"Damn. This is starting to unnerve me," Arnold said, cutting through the tape with his letter opener. "What the hell...,

Agggh!," he screamed, dropping the open container and its contents onto his desk while staggering backward.

Both men stared in disbelief. But it was Saunders who moved closer while Arnold, clinging to his leather chair, distanced himself from the package and its contents.

"I don't fucking believe it," Saunders said in a low, dry voice.

"Wha..., Wha..., What don't you believe?" Arnold shuddered. "They're real, aren't they? It's no joke, is it?" His complexion matched the gray sky.

"I'm afraid they are. If it's a joke, it's a damn grim one."

On the desk before them lay two small chunks of dry ice and two severed fingers, black blood caked to their fleshy stubs. The small, neatly sliced finger bones extruded beyond the shriveled flesh. Each finger sported a blood encrusted school ring.

"Looks like a male and a female finger," Saunders said, leaning closer. Arnold, meanwhile, brought his silk pocket handkerchief to his mouth as he bolted for his private bathroom, heaving his breakfast along the way. Ignoring the retching and flushing sounds, Saunders examined first the package and its markings more closely and then its grisly contents, moving each with the tip of Arnold's gold pen to avoid adding his fingerprints.

When Arnold returned the front of his tailored blue suit and silk tie bore tiny chunks of undigested bacon and sausage. His face, now drained of all color, matched his white mane. And his contrasting bloodshot eyes looked like two pee holes in the snow.
He had come back on unsteady legs and stayed far enough away from the desk to let Saunders know the problem was his to deal with, now.

"You'd better sit down, sir," his assistant said.

"Yes. Yes. I agree," he said, moving mechanically to his desk before realizing that was not where he wished to be at that moment.

Taking his arm, Saunders steered him to one of the soft armchairs grouped around the low coffee table across the room.

"What do you make of all this?" Arnold mumbled.

"I don't know, yet. But, I suspect we're about to find out."

Arnold gave him a puzzled look.

13

"In addition to the fingers," he explained, "there's a scrap of paper with a telephone number printed on it. I've looked through it all and there's nothing else."

"Then let's call the Swiss and find out what this horrendous thing's all about."

"I don't think the Swiss are going to be any help. It's not their number on the paper. In fact, it isn't a Cairo number. It seems to be a U. S. phone number. The area code is 410..., Maryland." As he said it, his expression changed and he exclaimed, "Shit!"

Returning to the desk, he rolled the fingers upright and said, hoarsely, "These are Naval Academy class rings!"

"Yes? What about them?"

"This morning's cables, sir. Did you see the terrorist summary?"

"No. I planned to get to it later. What about it?" he said, with a nervous glance at his desk.

"They found a professor's body. His throat was slit."

"And you think those are somehow connected?" He shifted uneasily in his chair.

"Gotta be. Let's see. Seven hours difference," Saunders calculated. "That'll make it five-thirty in the morning. I have a feeling time isn't going to be a factor. Whoever answers, I'm certain is going to be expecting this call."

Arnold stood and edged closer but said nothing as his assistant reached for the paper and the phone. Taking a deep breath, he dialed the number and waited. It was answered on the first ring.

"Superintendent's office," came the crisp military response.

"This is John Saunders calling for Ambassador Jennings Arnold from Cairo. The Ambassador wishes to speak with the Superintendent." He covered the mouthpiece with his hand and whispered, "I think it's best if you speak with him directly." Then, talking into the phone again, he asked, "What is his name please? Uh-uh," As he passed the phone to Arnold he said, "You'll be speaking to Rear Admiral Harold Harding, sir."

Arnold took the phone reluctantly, stretching the cord so as to keep as far from the fingers as possible. He waited only a few seconds.

"Hello, admiral. I have some distressing news...," He then went on to explain what had occurred as Saunders listened on the extension.

"Names? What names? There were no names, admiral."

"Inside the rings, Mr. Ambassador," came the response. "Would you kindly look inside and give me the names inscribed there."

It seemed to Saunders that Harding already knew the names and was seeking confirmation.

Arnold grew visibly weaker. He had no intention of touching the lifeless digits.

"Admiral, this is John Saunders on the extension. I'm number two at the embassy. This will take a moment. Please hold while we do as you ask."

As Arnold watched in stunned silence, Saunders put the phone down and stepped to the desk. And, holding the larger, male finger steady with the eraser end of a pencil, he slipped the letter opener beneath the ring and flipped it off the severed end then repeated the process with the female finger. Then, opening the desk drawer, he removed a carved ivory-handled magnifying glass and read the names.

"Sorry to have taken so long, admiral. I didn't wish to destroy any evidence," he finally said. "The names, sir, are Russell Bennett and Ingrid Lucerne."

Chapter Three

It was a few minutes before noon, nearly an hour after Arnold had received his package in Cairo, when CIA resident agent Bud Cassidy arrived at the Cafe El Greco on Rome's fashionable Via Condotti. He stepped inside and was greeted by the sweet aroma of coffee and the steady buzz of a hundred animated conversations. It was an ideal choice for a rendezvous. Someone in the crowd could be watching him but there was no way of picking them out. Whoever had lured him here knew what they were doing. The bar was packed two deep and every table was filled with impeccably dressed patrons but no one seemed interested in him. Finding a seat in the front room would be impossible but that wasn't where he needed to be. Edging forward, he pulled in his gut and sidestepped his way through the maze of *haute couture* to the back room, where he'd been instructed to go and wait.

He found a few empty tables and took one with a view of the entrance. Pushing the chair against the wall, he dropped down, pulled out his cigarettes and ordered an espresso. In truth, he was less curious about any intelligence he might pick up than in discovering who had directed him to this spot. Now close to retiring, the fifty-four year old veteran spy had lost the zest for these clandestine meetings, which were best left to the younger agents. Having earned his bones during the old Soviet regime, when ideology reigned over the mighty dollar, he was now having difficulty sorting out this new world order. With a price tag on everything today, he could easily imagine the discussion he'd be having in the next few minutes. A nervous stranger would offer information of dubious value in exchange for a hefty deposit in a neutral bank. It had all become so boring and predictable. Yet, because of that rare jewel that could make the other tedious encounters worthwhile, he had to be here. And, like the rest, there was no hint of how this one would go today. His only clue was the unnerving way the message had been delivered that morning.

He had been stopped at a traffic light, not far from the Coliseum, on the same route he'd taken to the embassy since moving into his apartment across town months earlier. It was one of those maddening Roman intersections where several main streets converge on a circle with traffic lights that never allow more than a few cars to pass before turning red again. Conscious of his personal security, he had tried alternating the commute using less traveled side streets but abandoned the idea soon after falling behind lumbering trash collectors and getting trapped by double parked delivery trucks. Had he truly been concerned for his safety he would have endured the inconvenience, but Bud Cassidy had lost his patience with the mundane world years ago. So, disregarding the dangers of following a predictable routine, he reverted to the speedier road that passed the Roman ruins. The many agents assassinated or kidnapped abroad because of similar indiscretions should have deterred him but Italy, especially Rome, gave one a false sense of security. Further, he believed he'd developed a sixth sense for such things and that would serve to protect him. But that was before the incident that morning.

Now, several hours later, as he crushed out one cigarette and lit another, he felt the gnawing uneasiness of one who could easily have been killed because of his carelessness. Not even the gun strapped firmly to his ankle lessened his anxiety. Recalling the encounter, perhaps for the hundredth time, he was thankful the helmeted motorcyclist had delivered a message rather than a grenade. He shuddered at the image of the stranger who had pulled up beside him. "Mr. Cassidy," he had said in a crisp, scornful voice, "this is for you." Then, offering an annoying grin, he shoved his gloved hand through the open window and dropped the note. It was over in a flash; before the light turned green. And while his attention was drawn to the paper the messenger sped away, leaving the seasoned agent behind in a cold sweat.

He took the note from his pocket and re-read it. *Be at Cafe El Greco at noon, alone. Take table in rear and wait. Urgent message will be delivered.* Typed and unsigned on standard bond paper, it gave no clue to the purpose of the meeting or who would be delivering the message. Again, he searched his memory of recent intel reports that might provide a hint but came up with nothing in the region that signified any urgency. He checked the time. It was twelve-ten. He'd wait another thirty minutes.

"Good afternoon, Mr. Cassidy." The accent was clearly middle eastern.

He looked up at the dark, wiry man. He had noticed him earlier in the bar and then watched him pass on his way to the rest room. Before he could respond the stranger slid into the chair that placed him closest to the door. He was young, probably in his early twenties, and as tense as a coiled spring.

"You have me at a disadvantage," Cassidy said in a casual tone.

"Names are not important." He shared the same sinister look as the man on the motorbike. "But, what I have to say is."

"Fair enough. Would you care for coffee?" Cassidy was about to signal the waiter but the man stopped him.

"Do not bother. This will not take long."

Cassidy shrugged, then took a cigarette and offered him one but it was refused. "Now, what can I do for you?" he said through the smoke.

The man nodded then began reciting what sounded like a memorized message. "It is imperative that you inform your government immediately that it must withdraw its naval and air forces from the Persian Gulf to a point well beyond striking range of Iran and it must do so within the next ten days."

Cassidy took a long drag while studying the man. "Is that it?" he finally asked.

"That is all there is, Mr. Cassidy." His expression suggested he was waiting for some acknowledgement the message would be forwarded. Evidently, that was part of his instructions.

Cassidy took another drag and wondered as he put the cigarette down, what purpose this meeting served. "Let me see if I got this right," he said, drawing out his words. "You expect the United States government to shift a major portion of its deployed forces on *your* say so?"

The man was sitting straight, not touching the chair back. From his pained expression, Cassidy could easily imagine he was thinking, *These Americans are so stupid. What is so difficult to understand?* Then, licking his lips, he repeated the demand, but much slower this time, as if he were addressing an imbecile.

The agent continued stalling. "You're not making this easy."

"What do you mean?" The youth was clearly puzzled.

"I'm flattered you guys think I have that kind of pull. But it just doesn't work that way."

"It must be done," he insisted. "You must convey the message."

Cassidy looked annoyed. "Come on, my friend. Is that why you went to the trouble of tracking me and luring me here? Let's be honest with each other. You really can't expect the United States to take your ultimatum seriously? Now, whatya say you cut the bullshit and tell me what you really want."

He watched the man flinch. If he was anything more than a courier, this was the time to come forward.

"Mr. Cassidy," he said stiffly, "you *must* take this message to your government. You have ten days from today to be out of striking range of Iran. There should be no mistaking this order."

"Order? Whose order!?"

"Just deliver the message. The rest will be made clear later. But now, you must deliver the message."

Cassidy snorted. "And if I do as you ask and my government refuses. Then what? Will Iran declare war on America?"

The man stared back in silence.

"Why should America relinquish its international right to the open seas? Or, for that matter, abrogate its treaty commitments? You see the problem, can't you? I will need answers to those questions. Because that's precisely what my superiors will want to know if I decide to pass on this ridiculous order of yours. If you can't provide some rationale, my friend, you're wasting your time."

Obviously agitated, he cleared his throat and said, more firmly, "For the last time, Mr. Cassidy. I repeat. Your country must withdraw its naval and air forces from the Persian Gulf. Out of striking range of Iran and it has ten days to do so."

With the rest of the day wide open, and knowing that couriers will generally repeat the message as long as they fear it isn't being received, Cassidy decided to see how far he could push him. In the interim he might pick up an extraneous bit of intel about the organization behind the demands.

"Can you work with me on this, pal? You know, give me a little something more that I can take back. A hint of what the hell's going on. Whatya say?"

The man shook his head in disbelief.

Cassidy leaned forward and said, "I tell you what, then. How 'bout I give you the phone number at the White House - you know, the boys in National Security - and you or one of your comrades can tell them yourself?"

Angered at Cassidy's taunting, the messenger said, "You are a very foolish man, Mr. Cassidy! Very foolish indeed. Do you think we make idle demands? You will learn otherwise." Suddenly, he was on his feet and reaching into his pocket. Cassidy's muscles tightened. Twice in one day he'd been caught off guard. To his relief, the man withdrew a wad of paper instead of a weapon. Holding it out, he said, "I repeat, Mr. Cassidy. Ten days." Then, tossing it at the agent, he turned and ran for the door.

Cassidy caught the heavy object and held it a moment before opening it. The moment he did, he remembered the terrorist summary sheet he'd read earlier. In the next instant he was shoving his way through the front room and scrambling for the door. Outside, he raised himself on his toes and, scanning the busy avenue, spotted the man at the foot of the Spanish Steps. He took off after him and knew as he crossed the congested piazza that he wasn't cut out for this. By the time he'd dodged several taxis and reached the broad steps he was breathing hard. Fortunately, the horde of tourists kept the man from making a straight run for it. But they also hampered Cassidy. Keeping the man in view, he began the long climb, zigzagging upward, taking two and three steps at a time when possible. He hadn't gone far when his calf muscles began tightening. Half way up his feet grew heavy and he was sucking in drafts of air to quell the burning in his lungs. Just when he thought he'd lose him, a gaggle of tourists appeared at the top, blocking the man's path. Confused, he turned to look back and Cassidy used the opportunity to gather his strength and propel himself upward. The man saw him and he spun and pushed through the crowd. Cassidy heard the angry shouts and prayed he could reach him before he made it to the street above. A moment later he heard a woman scream and saw the man rolling toward him, a dagger planted firmly in his neck.

* * *

(Washington, DC)

"Get me Admiral Harding on the phone," commanded the Director of the Central Intelligence Agency. Raymond Hemmings waited impatiently as he sat in his Georgetown study, clothed only in silk pajamas and a terry cloth robe while the call was patched from his home through the agency switchboard six miles away. Three minutes later the red light on his console lit up.

"Sir, I have Admiral Harding on the line." There was a faint click denoting the caller had left the secure line.

"Hunt, I have some unpleasant news." Hemmings was a retired four-star admiral and a Naval Academy alumnus. He had received a call from the duty officer twenty minutes earlier apologizing for disturbing him so early on Thanksgiving day before quickly summarizing the Rome incident and connecting the Director to Cassidy, who was standing in his office overlooking the Via Venetto.

Rear Admiral Harold "Hunt" Harding had not left the crisis command center he'd set up nearly fourteen hours earlier when Professor Nolan's body had been discovered and the ten midshipmen reported missing. With the efficiency gleaned from years of military experience, beginning with duty in Vietnam and concluding with a tour in the Persian Gulf prior to reporting to the academy, Harding, with the blessing of the Chief of Naval Operations, had immediately moved to take control of the Navy's role in the terrorist plot. From the onset, the CNO had seen the wisdom of Harding's advice; to keep a lid on the incident and subsequent investigation by activating a command center at the naval station, across the Severn River from the academy and directing operations from there. Both men had convinced General Lucerne and the Secretary of Defense that keeping it out of Washington during this early stage was critical if they wished to avoid turning the crisis into a media frenzy.

"What is it, Ray?" His usually resonant voice was weak and hoarse. Mobilizing the Navy's resources had kept him up all night. With no emerging clues and his energy depleted by worry for the mids', he'd begun sinking into a slump, only to be jolted back by the call from Cairo. Now, an hour later, having digested the gruesome news of the amputated fingers, he steeled himself for yet another blow.

"Our agent in Rome has been contacted. We know what's driving this ugly thing now but we don't know why. Iran has given us an ultimatum to withdraw our forces from the Gulf in ten days."

"You think that's why our mids have been kidnapped?"

Harding was having difficulty making the connection. Rather, he wished it weren't so. But the grim news he'd received from Cairo earlier certainly indicated they had become unwilling pawns in an international power play.

"'Fraid so shipmate. Our man was presented with a nasty signature to the demand."

"Oh, God," he cried. "Not another finger, Ray." Harding's voice conveyed the profound sorrow of a parent.

"Just the ring this time," Hemmings responded, heavily. "But," he added remorsefully, "there was blood on it." He went on to confirm the name inside and informed the superintendent it was on its way to the agency as they spoke.

* * *

Trish Mathews had been at her desk at *The Washington Post* since eight-thirty putting the finishing touches on the second of a two-part series on military base closures. She'd spent most of October working the story on the Hill, interviewing members of the Senate and House Armed Services committees as well as congressional members whose districts were being threatened by the third round of closings. Then, in November, she hit the road, visiting many of the bases with the goal of assessing the impact on local communities.

She'd been covering the Pentagon for more than a year since being transferred from the northern Virginia city desk. As the junior member of the *Post's* Pentagon team she had to suffer the indignities of working what she considered tedious issues because the man who headed the defense beat, Barney Solomon, a crusty old reporter who'd been with the paper more than thirty-five years, insisted that she earn her wings, just as he had. She soon learned that earning one's wings meant accompanying Marines on field maneuvers through swamps and deserts, parachuting with Rangers and enduring 100+ degree temperatures in the unsteady bowels of rolling ships. Solomon had maintained that if she aspired to his job, she had better know how expensive weapons and equipment was used in the field before accepting the bullshit in the thousands of press releases cranked out at military headquarters.

"Once you're ensconced in this five-sided loony bin," he'd told her on her first day, "it's easy to get caught up in Pentagon politics. Unfortunately for the squids and grunts who put their lives on the line everyday, too many politicians here don't have a clue about what life is like out where the rubber meets the road. That's where we come in. But, you're going to have to be careful. These bureaucrats love wining and dining you while blowing smoke up your pretty, little ass so you'll dutifully go out and write the crap they feed you. Then, afterwards, they'll tell you what a great reporter you are and you'll believe them. It's all a game, Trish," he had cautioned. "The secret is to get out there and find the real heroes," he'd counseled her, "and, when you're back in the Pentagon, the phonies will stick out a mile."

At first she had gone reluctantly to where Solomon had sent her, but soon she realized the old bastard was wiser than she'd given him credit. Now, thinking about the Thanksgiving dinner she was missing with her friends as she struggled to meet her deadline, she looked at the clock above the editor's office. It was noon. She noted sourly that Solomon was home with his family in Pennsylvania for the holiday weekend, then reprimanded herself as she reflected that he had earned the time off by missing many more holidays than she'd experienced in her short life span. Nevertheless, at twenty-six, far from her family in Michigan and alone in a quiet newsroom, Trish was feeling homesick and more than a little sorry for herself when her phone rang.

"Miss Mathews?"

"Yes. This is she."

"Oh. Good. I was hoping you'd be at your desk."

"Yes. Unfortunately, I am," she said, pleased to play the martyr. "With whom am I speaking?"

"That's not important, Miss Mathews. I am but a messenger."

Oh, great! she thought. Just what I need, an anonymous caller. She sighed and said with a hint of displeasure, "Well, what may I do for you, today?"

"It's more, what I can do for you," he countered.

His tone was even and friendly and she put him in his thirties. Maybe early forties.

"All right, then. What can you do for me?"

"You have an opportunity to become a player in a complex and dangerous series of negotiations, Miss Mathews. Do you think you are up to the task?"

"Look. If this is one of the guys on the paper, fuck off. I'm not here today because I want to be. I've got work to do." She was about to hang up.

"This is no joke, Miss Mathews." Suddenly, he was more business-like.

"Okay," she said warily. "I'll bite. What's the scoop?" She reached over and pushed the caller ID button and noted he'd blocked the number.

"You're about to become part of the story of the century. But you're going to have to be a little more cordial, Trish."

She stiffened at the unexpected use of her first name. Not only was it intrusive but it made her feel he knew more about her than just her name. She looked around the newsroom and then out the window to the building across the street.

"Sorry. I didn't mean to jump at you," she said, regretting her outburst. "It wasn't at all professional. I'm all ears. Please continue."

"That's better, Trish. When this is over, you won't be working anymore holidays," he said, becoming more conciliatory. "There's been an incident at the Naval Academy. Yesterday, a professor was found murdered, his throat slit."

She gasped but he seemed not to notice.

"I know what you're thinking," he continued. "There's no way the Navy could be sitting on that story. And since you ain't heard about it, it couldn't have happened. Right?"

"Absolutely," she agreed. "And that's why I'm going to hang up."

"Well, it did happen, Trish. I guarantee it. And what also happened that you haven't heard is the kidnapping of ten midshipmen."

"Okay, mister! The joke's over and I have work to do," she said in a show of Irish temper.

"Don't hang up, Trish," he commanded. "I know it sounds crazy. But I want you to hear me out and then, if you still think it's a joke...,"

"This is incredible," she cut in. "Don't you have anything better to do? A football game to watch or something?"

"Trish. Just listen. Stay with me," he said patiently. "Okay? You with me?"

"Yeah. Yeah. I'm here," she said. "But I don't know why."

"You won't be sorry," he promised. "Yesterday, at one-forty pm," he began, "ten mids were taken from their classroom in Rickover Hall. Their professor was murdered and his body left behind. The mids were snapped up for two reasons. One is to avenge the deaths caused by the downing of an Iranian airliner by the USS Vincenes. I'm sure you remember that. The other, is to force the United States to withdraw its naval and air forces from the Persian Gulf region within ten days."

She was writing as he spoke.

"The ultimatum to withdraw has been delivered. And, no doubt has already reached the highest offices. But the reason for the demand hasn't been made. And that's the purpose of this call. We want you to deliver the reason. Can you do that for us, Trish?" His tone had changed again, as if he were taking her into his confidence.

"First tell me the reason."

"Fair enough. Iran intends to invade its longtime enemy, Iraq, and it doesn't want interference from America or its allies. It must be now, because there is irrefutable proof Saddam Hussein is preparing to use his re-stockpiled biological and chemical weapons against them, just as he did during the seventy-nine war, as well as on the Kurds in northern Iraq and the rebels along the Tigris and Euphrates rivers in the south. In sum, Iran sees this as an opportunity to rescue its spiritual brothers while eliminating its old enemy. Admittedly, some will see it as a move to establish regional hegemony, but I assure you, it's purely a preemptive strike. That's it in a nutshell."

"How noble," she said. "And the professor? Did he have to die?"

He clicked his tongue in a suggestive manner. "War is never pretty. He was a necessary casualty. Now. Will you deliver the message?"

"If what you say is true, I don't understand why you're coming to me."

"What difference does that make? Right now, the only thing you got to think about is that this story fell into your lap. My advice is to take it and run with it. Chances are, it'll never happen again."

"To whom do you want me to carry this message?" she asked, wanting to believe him.

"Atta girl."

She winced. She hated that expression.

"We want you to take it through proper channels. You know, the military way," he said with a humorless laugh. "Call the Superintendent of the Naval Academy and tell him, if the U.S. fails to comply with the ultimatum his ten midshipmen will die ten days from today and," here his voice turned icy, "it won't be nice. He'll take it from there. It's that easy."

She felt sick. "Is there anything I can do - I mean, the paper can do - to help those midshipmen?"

"Don't worry about the mids, Miss Mathews. They'll be fine as long as everybody does what they're told, including you."

"This so bizarre."

"Look on the bright side. You're on your way to a Pulitzer. Isn't that the name of the game?"

She didn't answer but looked around, hoping someone had entered.

"Oh. Before calling the Supe, you'd better pick up the Thanksgiving gift at the reception desk in the lobby. It'll make your call to Annapolis much more credible. Bye for now, sweet pea."

"Wait! Wait!" she implored but he had already hung up.

Ten minutes later she was back at her desk, the blood stained class ring before her. She stared at it for a long while, alternating between imagining the terror the mids were going through and writing the lead paragraph of the story. Finally, she reached over and lifted the phone. The operator answered immediately. "United States Naval Academy. How may I help you?"

"Public Affairs Office, please." As she waited she poked nervously at the ring with her pencil.

The phone was picked up on the second ring. "Lieutenant Commander Veltri speaking."

There was nothing in his calm manner to suggest the school was under siege and she wondered again if this was an ugly joke.

"Jim, this is Trish Mathews. I'm surprised you're in today," she said, hoping to draw him out. "I thought I'd get the duty officer."

"Well, you know how it is in this business, Trish. Always something. What can I do for you on this day of Thanksgiving?"

"I've just had a strange phone call. Frankly, I hope it was a crank but..., Well, you know..., We have to follow up on these things."

"Sure," he said.

"It's about a dead professor and some missing mids," she blurted. There was a long silence and suddenly the phone felt very heavy in her hand.

When Veltri replied his voice was low and somber. "Trish, you caught me by surprise." He had taken the call not in his office, in the admin building on campus, but in the command center across the river. And now he was waiting for the admiral to pick up the extension. "What exactly do you know?"

So, it was true, she thought with mixed emotions. Centering her notes before her, she licked her parched lips and repeated what the caller had told her. She concluded by describing the ring that had been left for her, and saying, "I think I need some answers, Jim."

"And you shall have them, Miss Mathews." The unfamiliar voice startled her. "This is Rear Admiral Harding, Miss Mathews. I've been listening."

Now, suppressing a rush of excitement, she said, "Hello, admiral. What can you tell me about this situation?"

"Miss Mathews," he began slowly, "I fear you have become unwittingly embroiled in matters of the highest national security. Based on what you've told us, I must insist that you come to Annapolis immediately, where, I promise, I will tell you all that we know. The only thing I ask in return is that you not discuss this with anyone prior to coming here. Please, Miss Mathews," he implored, "I know this is a big story for you but I ask that you remember we have the lives of ten young midshipmen at stake. You'll get everything you want," he repeated. "Just please keep a lid on it for now. May I count on your confidentiality?"

The notion of a Pulitzer was dizzying. She had to call her editor. The story was too big. But, there were the midshipmen to consider. And, like it or not, she was part of the story and not just an objective reporter. She looked down at the bloodied ring and, praying she was making the right decision, she consented.

"Thank you, Miss Mathews," Harding said with noticeable relief. "I will have a car outside your office in five minutes to bring you here." Then, sensing her predicament, he added, "You have done the right thing."

29

Chapter Four

"I agree. Red Cell should head up the rescue op," Marine Corps General John Lucerne told the Chief of Naval Operations from his windowless post in the National Military Command Center. "You have my concurrence to bring them aboard. I also support your decision to have Hunt run the op," he said, referring to Admiral Harding. Then, as he was about to hang up, he added, "And, Lloyd, give him my best. I know he's under a lot of pressure."

The two flag officers were in regular contact since it fell to Admiral Lloyd Jeffries to notify Lucerne of his daughter's kidnapping. Now, as he prepared to activate the Navy's elite counter-terrorist team, Jeffries thought of the grisly disclosures and the demoralizing effect they must be having on Lucerne and he prayed for his friend. Fortunately, the Iranians had misjudged the general, who, in spite of the trauma, was refusing to buckle. But he was only one factor in the equation. There was also Bennett and the president.

Disregarding his own troubles, Lucerne plunged into the task of providing the president with a military option for dissuading Iran's Fundamentalist regime from attacking its neighbor. Working with the other services, he and his joint staff plotted the disposition of every deployed unit, its readiness level and response time. Regrettably, with U.S. forces half of what they were when General Colin Powell directed Desert Storm in 1991, his options were limited. Nevertheless, by six o'clock that evening he was prepared to make his case at the hastily called National Security Council meeting. Settling into his limo, he headed for the White House with several options as well as the latest intelligence assessments of Iran's ability to conduct a successful attack and Iraq's ability to defend itself. Now, with a few minutes to himself, he stared out at the quiet city and for the first time that day imagined the mind set of the terrorists and how his resolute daughter was coping with what had to be very difficult conditions. It was not the most heartening image.

His driver pulled into the underground garage of a glass-fronted office building on 17th Street, across from the White House. From there, Lucerne made his way through a pedestrian tunnel to the Old Executive Office building and into the White House basement. It was a route used whenever the president and his aides wished to avoid prying eyes, as they did today. Inside the NSC conference room the mood was hushed but intense. Louis Mack, the vice president, was huddled to one side with CIA Director Hemmings and Gerard Diamond, head of the National Security Council, while pockets of aides and lesser notables carried on their own spirited conversations. The casual attire of everyone but Mack and Hemmings suggested they'd been called back in from their holiday. Standing ramrod straight in his pressed Marine uniform, the 6'4" general generated a commanding presence as entered.

Mack was first to respond. Looking up, the vice president broke from the others and rushed over to him. "John," he said, grasping Lucerne's hand, "I am terribly distraught by this horrible act of violence. Bea joins me in extending our prayers to you and your family."

Lucerne liked Mack. He was an honest and intelligent man, who could be counted on to provide an unbiased opinion when one was needed. "Thank you, Mr. Vice President. I appreciate your kind thoughts. I'll be sure to pass them on to Miriam. She's taking it quite badly, as you might expect."

"No doubt," Mack said. Then, addressing the military commander and not the grieving parent, he said, "I'll do whatever I can to support you."

Lucerne nodded. "It's appreciated. From what I hear we may have our work cut out for us."

Now it was Diamond's turn. Approaching the general, the shorter man extended his hand and lamented, "Please accept my heartfelt sympathy for the agony you and your family must be enduring as this senseless act of savagery unfolds." As he spoke, his voice rose and his face reddened. Then, on the brink of trembling, he said, "It's scandalous that those barbarians should violate our sovereign territory. First the World Trade Center and now..., They've stepped over the line, general. As soon as your daughter and the others are safe, those fuckers will pay. We'll teach `em a lesson they'll never forget."

Lucerne didn't dislike the former anti-war activist, but he never really took to him, either. Now, he simply nodded at his bellicose ranting.

Next, came Hemmings. And while this wasn't their first discussion that day, it was their first meeting since the kidnapping and it gave him an opportunity to say in person what he'd said earlier. "John, I'm sorry about this. They've done a horrible deed." There was no mistaking the grief in his eyes.

As they spoke the door slid open and J. Farnsworth Harrison, the Deputy Secretary of State, strode in with Senator Bennett, who looked pitifully drawn and tired.

Lucerne and Hemmings stood aside as Mack consoled the beleaguered politician. Then, as their eyes met, Lucerne stepped forward and an uneasy silence fell upon the room. Those with a seasoned eye, like Hemmings, noted a hint of tension between the two men while the others saw only two distraught parents.

At six-forty, five minutes before the president was to arrive, they all drifted to their places at the long table and waited. No one commented as the appointed time arrived and passed. Waiting for the tardy president was common and Lucerne fumed as he wondered if Leslie Pickens would be late if it were his daughter that had been kidnapped.

Finally, at five of seven, the chief of staff entered and announced, "Gentlemen. The President."

Pickens rushed in behind him as if attending a fund raiser. "Howdy, boys. Sorry to be late," he called out with a flourish. "You know how it is." Then, seeing Bennett across the room he dropped the smile and moved quickly to him. "Russ," he said, as he approached and extended his hand. "What a terrible, terrible thing. I can't begin to tell you how sorry I am. You can rest assured, ol' buddy, we're going to pull out the stoppers on this one. Those cocksuckers ain't getting away with this. No, siree," he said, squeezing his mentor's shoulder.

Then, to Lucerne, he said, "General, I am equally devastated for you and your family. Mrs. Pickens and I share your suffering."

"Thank you, Mr. President," he replied, clasping the fleshy hand of the man who stood in sharp moral and physical contrast to him, a fact which didn't go unnoticed by the others, including the proud, young Marine who had escorted Pickens from his quarters.

While they were both of equal height there was little similarity between them. Ten years younger than Lucerne and pear shaped, Pickens embodied the undisciplined lifestyle of his generation. In a constant flutter, he was an ink blot in motion. To his colleagues, the core of elite Washingtonians, who had expected more from the leader of the free world, his antics were often a cause of uneasiness. Standing beside him in sharp contrast, with his graying yellow hair trimmed to corps standards, broad shoulders and flat stomach, Lucerne embodied the strength and determination of a battle-tested soldier. Unlike Pickens, he spoke and moved with monk-like precision.

Uncomfortable with the disparity, Pickens extracted his hand and said, "I guess we'd better get down to business."

As NSC Director, it was Diamond's show and so he began when everyone was seated. "Mr. President, though you have already been briefed as events of this tragic drama have unfolded, I think we should review them in the order in which they occurred for the benefit of everyone present."

Pickens nodded while plucking two chocolate chip cookies from the platter set out by the mess stewards. With that, Diamond filled in the excruciating details of what they had learned from each of the terrorists' disclosures, concluding with Trish Mathews' visit to the Naval Academy and admiral Harding's assurances that she had agreed not to discuss the matter in exchange for an exclusive on the story.

"Can she be trusted?" Pickens asked.

Bennett answered from the opposite end of the table before Diamond could. "I'll vouch for her. She's been a long time friend of both Frances and me. In fact," he cleared his throat, "at this moment she's with my wife at our home." It wasn't necessary, but he added, "She's as devastated as we are."

"She'll have one helluva story when this is over," Pickens added. Then, to no one in particular, he asked, "Why do you think she was brought into this thing?"

Hemmings responded. "We think they've planned this operation down to every detail. Nothing they do is without purpose."

"So, you're saying they specifically targeted *Russ'* class?" Bennett interrupted.

"It seems that way, senator," the CIA director replied. "It was evident as soon as they delivered the first package in Cairo. The rest confirms it, including the professional way the messenger was killed in Rome. We're certain it's all aimed at two people in this room," he said with a nod at both of the affected parents. It was a theory he had shared earlier with Lucerne and which the Marine also subscribed to.

"But what about the Mathews girl?" Pickens asked. "How's she fit in?"

"Aside from her relationship to the Bennetts, which can't be discounted," Hemmings went on, "bringing the news media in on this is yet another way of keeping the pressure on us."

"You mean, we're supposed to think they'll blow this thing wide open by contacting other news media?" the president asked.

Hemmings nodded. It bothered him that the newswoman was in contact with Bennett, particularly since he didn't know yet where he stood.

"How about you, John? Do you agree with that notion?" Bennett asked Lucerne.

"Yes. I don't believe it was a coincidence that they targeted that class," he replied somberly. Then, more slowly, he said, "What also bothers me are the other implications."

"Whatdya mean?" Pickens asked.

"Well, I don't wish to get ahead of the CIA on that. It's something they've given more consideration to than I have. As you know, Mr. President, I've been occupied with other areas."

"Yes, of course," Pickens said. Turning to Hemmings, he asked, "What about it, Ray? What implications?" He reached for another cookie.

The agenda was proceeding as he and Lucerne had intended, and Hemmings replied, "It's evident the Iranians are employing psychological warfare, Mr. President."

"Psychological warfare? What the hell for?" Pickens retorted.

"They want to influence you. Your friendship with Senator Bennett is no secret." He measured his words to avoid suggesting what he suspected; that Bennett might put his son's welfare above the nation's. Nor could he disclose his other misgivings without alienating Pickens and some of the others around the table.

"What about General Lucerne?" Pickens asked. "You haven't mentioned him."

"That's the other aspect of this operation that suggests considerable preparation. You may recall, several months ago the chairman's office announced that General Loveland had been diagnosed with operable prostate cancer, which would be treated at Walter Reed in the fall. It's obvious the Iranians took that into consideration. No other group of midshipmen would produce this effect," he said, acknowledging Bennett and Lucerne. "Mr. President, this phase of their operation has been extremely well-planned and well-executed. In addition to hitting us close to home, the Iranians are making every effort to influence your decision."

"This phase?" Pickens asked.

"There is the matter of attacking Iraq," Hemmings reminded him.

"Wait a minute!" Bennett interrupted. "Aren't we getting ahead of ourselves, here? I'm getting the impression that you've already made up your mind not to accede to their ultimatum. As if that were the logical course of action."

Hemmings bristled. "Senator, are you suggesting that we role over on this one?"

"Don't put words in my mouth," he cautioned. "Maybe you've already bought into the notion that we're gonna fight `em on this but I for one haven't. Nor have my colleagues on the Hill. Further, I haven't heard anything to indicate the president has. No, sir. As I see it, it ain't a done deal. Not from where I'm sitting."

Hemmings glanced at Lucerne. They were losing ground before they had established a foothold. "And just where are you sitting?" he pressed Bennett.

Hemmings was no longer addressing Bennett the victim, but rather the powerful and oftentimes ruthless politician. It was no secret that many around the table feared him, including the president. "Well, I can tell you where I'm *not* sitting. And that is with those who believe the only option is to deny the Iranians what they are seeking. This issue is far too complex for us to rush headlong into without first examining all the options." Then offering a twisted smile, he added, "Not that I ain't opposed to kicking some ass once we get our midshipmen back." Turning to Pickens, he said, "Mr. President, I think we must consider our alternatives very carefully. Iran's decision to attack Iraq poses some very interesting issues which we ought not dismiss out of hand."

Hemmings tensed. Bennett, who was not a member of the NSC, had been invited at the president's urging because of his son's involvement in the kidnapping. Now, the focus had shifted and Bennett, rather than the NSC, was setting the agenda. This was not good for the home team.

Pickens nodded at his friend and said, "I agree. We can't afford to be rash. And, in that regard, we certainly welcome your input, Russ. Won't you please continue."

Chapter Five

Commander Tom Sampson, the Navy SEAL who headed Red Cell, had more than a professional interest in the kidnapping. As a fourth generation academy alumnus and the great grandson of Rear Admiral William Thomas Sampson, whose long and distinguished career included Academy Superintendent, Chief of the Bureau of Ordnance and Commander-in-Chief, U. S. Naval Forces North Atlantic Station during the 1898 war with Spain, he took the terrorists' intrusion personally. Duke, as he was known among his peers because of his resemblance to John Wayne, welcomed the opportunity to use his combat skills and those of his fellow commandos to find and destroy the scumbags who had taken and mutilated the midshipmen.

He was the first of his team to arrive at Harding's command center in Annapolis, where he began immediately analyzing the evidence gathered by the Naval Investigative Service. The NIS agent in charge explained that the trail of evidence indicated the mids had been taken from Rickover Hall to a waiting van and subsequently driven off the grounds to Pirates' Cove, a little-used marina off a county road, just eight miles south of Annapolis. The van which, he said had been found abandoned there, had been turned over to FBI forensics. It was his opinion that the hostages had been put aboard a fast boat, most likely for further transfer to a ship off the Maryland or Virginia coast. Sampson listened without commenting. The seasoned warrior had learned to never accept the obvious, as some of his less cautious shipmates had when encountering booby traps during special combat ops. Instead, he thanked the agent and went in to see the admiral.

"Welcome aboard, Tom," Harding said in a tired and strained tone. Wasting no time, he said, "The ground rules are simple. Unless otherwise directed, we're handling this as a covert op from beginning to end. As we speak, General Lucerne is preparing to brief the president and the NSC and he's told me he intends to urge them to hold that course."

Sampson looked doubtful. And he asked, "What do you think our chances are of keeping a lid on this?

"We have to try. In spite of their grief, Professor Nolan's family is willing to state that he died of natural causes. They understand our dilemma and have agreed to do whatever's necessary to rescue our mids. The Mathews girl has also agreed to sit on the story. And, as far as the brigade's concerned, we've got three days until classes resume before we have to address their classmates' absences. Since the ten are in different companies, I'll vary the reasons and no one will make the connection. I'm counting on the activities leading up to next week's game with Army to deflect everyone's attention."

"And the Iranian demands to withdraw our forces? How's that going to be handled?"

"That's above my pay grade," Harding said, "but Lucerne isn't concerned about that. Not yet, anyway. Of course, whatever decision is made will have to be coordinated with our allies. If we're lucky they'll support us."

Again, Sampson expressed his misgivings. "With the way Pickens has managed to piss off the French and the Brits, I wouldn't be so confident if I were Lucerne."

"Emergencies rekindle old friendships. Let's hope that holds true now. Given their cooperation, I think we can handle the situation in the gulf - that is, if the president buys off on it."

"Buys off? You think he has other plans?" Sampson asked with surprise.

"You never know with him. There is the Bennett factor." Then, changing the subject, he said, "Right now, my primary concern is getting our mids back safely. That's all you have to be concerned about. I hope your guys are in shape, because they're going to have to work around the clock."

"Don't worry. We're up to it."

Harding looked hard at him. "Let's hope so. For now, you answer to no one but me. Whatever DoD assets you need are at your disposal. We've got to find those kids and bring `em out safely," he stressed. "You understand?"

Sampson nodded. "We'll find them, admiral. And, we'll bring them home." What he didn't say, is that he intended to take no prisoners.

"There's no room for failure, Tom. There has to be a clear message sent. We can't let those bastards get away with this." Sampson had known the admiral a long time and never once heard him swear.

By seven that evening all fifteen SEALs were at the command center armed and ready to go or to do whatever their leader required. Earlier, at Sampson's request, the Chief of Personnel had sent a series of priority messages to selected Navy commands detaching an additional fifteen SEALs all of whom were personally known to Sampson, and assigning them without explanation to Red Cell. All had served with him before. Most were in the U.S., a few overseas would arrive the following day.

Now, with the nucleus of his team present, he gathered them to one side, away from the curious eyes of the others manning the high security complex. Out of habit they were a secretive group of unconventional warriors, who had exchanged their uniforms for civilian clothes and wore their hair unkept and their beards scruffy. Only Sampson and his assistant, Lieutenant Commander Cort McLeod, the team's two leaders, conformed to the Navy's strict grooming standards. The others, for good reason, looked more like the terrorists they hunted. The only uniformity in their attire was their non-uniformity. At first glance they resembled a ragtag band of misfits, as might be found on society's fringes. Up close, they exuded a quiet confidence that could easily unnerve someone with lesser combat skills. Individually, they were chameleons. Together, they were a lethal and effective counter-force.

With the door to the small office closed and his men in a semi-circle around him - some straddling chairs, others cross-legged on the tiled floor or leaning against the wall - Sampson repeated everything he'd learned since being called in, including the evidence gathered by the Naval Investigators. While sketchy, it provided a datum from which to analyze the terrorists. At around nine, Sampson sent his assistant to the Office of Naval Intelligence.

"Cort," he said, "see what they have on merchant shipping in and out of Baltimore within the past week; including their current locations and destinations and scheduled ports of call. We're also going to need a list of ships that sailed near the Chesapeake Bay entrance within the preceding twenty-four hours. As soon as you get it give a copy to NSA. I'll alert them to expect you."

"Why the National Security Agency?" the NIS agent asked.

"To monitor their comms," he explained.

There was a knock at the door as he spoke and a young Marine guard poked his head in. "Commander, there's someone here to see you."

Standing behind him was a fellow who looked more like an insurance salesman than a cop. As Sampson looked at him, he held up his FBI ID and said, "Floyd Cutler, commander. I believe you're expecting me."

"Welcome aboard, Mr. Cutler. It was good of the bureau to provide a liaison. We appreciate it," he said.

This was Cutler's first assignment with the Navy and he looked a little apprehensive as he stepped inside and surveyed the men with their sidearms.

"We're not your standard Navy SEAL team," Sampson said, noting the agent's expression. "But don't let it fool you."

He cleared his throat. "They tell me at the bureau you're a crazy bunch of bastards but you're also the best."

Sampson smiled. "I believe the first part but I'd be surprised if the bureau thinks anybody's better than them. Thanks anyway." Then, more seriously, he asked, "So, what've you got for us?"

"The preliminary report on the evidence gathered from the van," he said, handing Sampson a thin file.

He read it quickly. "This doesn't tell us much, except that at some time the mids were in the van."

"You have problems with that?" the FBI agent asked.

Sampson took a moment to spit tobacco juice into an empty coke can he kept handy. "Maybe. If it supports the notion that they were taken to Pirates' Cove."

"Well, that's what the evidence suggests," Cutler said.

"It sure does. And I guess we're supposed to conclude they were put on a boat which ferried them to a merchant heading out of the country."

"That was our theory."

"Yours and the boys at NIS."

"You don't buy it, commander?" Cutler asked.

"I'm having some difficulty."

"Would you care to share it?"

"Who're you working for, Cutler?"

"Why, you of course. Look, commander. I'm here to help you, not hinder you or do an end run on you. My marching orders were to support you any way we can. That's no bullshit."

"Okay. But a word of warning, my friend. You guys try getting out ahead of me on this and I'll personally cut your nuts off. Got it?"

Cutler smiled. "I wanna keep my nuts."

"These guys are obviously pros," Sampson began. "To me, that suggests they left nothing to chance."

"So?"

"So. Once you start adding it all up, this Pirate's Cove thing doesn't ring true."

"A red herring?"

Sampson nodded. "First, there's the problem of logistics. When ten mids leave their classroom in the middle of the day without attracting somebody's attention it tells me they walked out willingly. No coercion. That also means they didn't see the professor murdered. So, somebody had to stay behind to take care of him. Even if they left willingly, at some point during the transit phase they're going to figure out what's going on. And from what I know of mids, they can get downright hostile once they think somebody's fuckin' with them. To be prepared for that, the bad guys had to have enough men to control the mids. Say one for every two mids. They also had to establish a perimeter with lookouts. And everybody's got to be connected by radio. And if they're pros they're going to have a lead car and a tail car. And that's just to get everybody safely away from here. You see what I'm getting at?"

Cutler nodded.

"So, where are the other cars? There's nothing in your report about other traffic at the marina. Just the van. What happened to the other cars and their passengers? To make a mid-day transfer from the van to the boat without attracting attention you have to move fast and quietly.

"Then there's the boat. They needed one large enough to accommodate at least fifteen passengers and a crew and it had to be fast enough to travel a great distance without refueling. We're talking a damn big boat." Picking up the FBI report, he asked, "So, where's the reference to the boat? There's nothing here about a boat."

Cutler didn't answer.

"Next," Sampson said, "let's consider the time line." He was at his best when dissecting problems. Sitting on the edge of the gray metal desk, he said, "The kidnappers came and left with the mids without being detected, which means they made their move when the halls were empty - when classes were in session. So, I'm guessing they gave themselves about a thirty minute window at most. Somewhere between one-fifteen and one-forty-five. Okay. Now, they're in the van with mids. Everybody's all happy and they take off for Pirates' Cove using the main roads and holding to the speed limit. They don't want to get caught speeding with that cargo, who by then have probably begun suspecting something. That would put them at the marina at approximately two-fifteen to two-twenty-five, depending on how many lights they caught along the way."

"You're pretty sure of that?" Cutler asked.

"It took me twenty-five minutes today," Sampson replied. "But there wasn't much traffic because of the holiday. Now, according to your report, there are no traces of blood; either in the van or anywhere at the marina. That tells me the fingers had to be severed afterwards. Nor, does your report indicate any signs of a struggle in the vicinity."

The agent nodded. "That's no surprise. Pros don't usually injure or harm hostages during the travel phase of the takedown unless they have to assert control over them. An injured hostage will only slow you down."

Sampson agreed. "Those fingers were part of the plan and probably didn't come off until they reached a permanent or semi-permanent hideout. So, getting back to the first phase of the takedown, the distance from the marina to the mouth of the bay is over a hundred and twenty miles. To reach the open seas, you're looking at a ten to twelve hour boat ride at a sustained speed of fifteen knots or more with good weather."

"That's doable," the agent countered.

"These guys put a lot of effort into planning this op. It seems foolish to go to that much trouble and risk it all on an unexpected change in the weather. And even if they did decide to throw the dice with the weather, it's still unlikely. They had to know the mids would be discovered missing during evening meal formation, at the latest. That's four hours after they took them! Even though it was dark, they'd be less than half way down the Chesapeake with a six to eight hour transit still ahead of them. I sure as hell wouldn't want to be out there on a large boat, speeding toward the Atlantic with the Navy going to general quarters. It's too risky."

"Sure. For you. But you aren't an Iranian. They do things differently, and that includes taking unnecessary risks. How the hell would you characterize this whole operation, if not risky?"

Sampson liked Cutler's intensity but he wished he had more experience. But then, he reminded himself, the bureau didn't have the same experience as Red Cell. "The next problem has to do with transporting the fingers. To arrive at the embassy by noon, they had to be taken to an airport for a ten hour, non-stop flight, that is, unless they used the Concorde." He shook his head, "Ain't too many international airports along the Chesapeake that I know of. And, the last time I checked, the Concorde doesn't land at any of them. So, once you start working the problem backwards, from the time the package was delivered in Cairo, you realize how tight their schedule was. They used the fingers and the school rings plus the noon delivery times as a signature to verify the
45

authenticity of their messages and they held to it. For the life of me, I don't know how they could've met those self-imposed deadlines by going to sea. But then," he said with a shrug, "we don't have all the answers yet. He reached for his soda can and spit.

Chapter Six

Pickens had been woefully unprepared for the NSC meeting and was now regretting having let it proceed so long. By not taking control at the outset, he had allowed it to turn into a three-ring circus. As a consequence, the issue of how to respond to the Iranians had become polarized. He was furious with himself for naively thinking everyone would be in agreement. Instead, battle lines had been drawn; with Bennett arguing in favor of complying with Iran's demands and Lucerne adamantly opposed. It had been a terrible ordeal and he still felt the stress of being pushed and pulled by both sides.

Now, reclused in the sanctity of the Oval Office, he struggled with what he knew were convincing arguments for and against acceding to the Iranians. It was a dilemma that left him anxious and unsettled. Given a choice he would have bet his last dollar before stepping into the briefing room that both Bennett and Lucerne would have argued forcefully for taking whatever action was necessary to ensure the safety of their children and the other mids. But, to his astonishment, Lucerne insisted that the right course was not to capitulate, which made Bennett assert, Pickens thought rather convincingly, that the Iranians were actually doing us a favor by attacking Saddam Hussein.

What further vexed him was the short fuse on this bomb. Making a life and death decision was bad enough but having to do it quickly, without benefit of proper counsel was proving difficult. Aware that he was already into the second day of the ten day countdown, he wished he could gather his young staffers around for an all-nighter in which they could game it, just as they had done with other issues, albeit less pressing ones. But the Iranians had allowed no time for that nor could he bring his team into the discussion without having the messy problem leak out to the world, an eventuality, which he knew all too well, would create an enormous amount of pressure on him. In that regard, he had to agree with Lucerne when he'd asserted the need to keep the entire incident under wraps.

"What're we gonna' do?" he asked, wearily, without turning to face the man seated across the desk from him, preferring instead the expansive view of the south lawn and the Ellipse, dominated by the Washington Monument beyond. "They both make strong arguments," he offered while raising the mug he'd been cradling in his lap and sipping from it.

Daren McCurdy never thought when he accepted the chief of staff post six months earlier, the third man to hold the job in this tumultuous administration in as many years, that he'd be guiding his boss through such rough terrain. And, like Pickens, his head ached over the implications of taking either course. As one who had come to Washington on Pickens' coattails, he knew he wasn't qualified commenting on matters of such import. There were legions of more skilled people who were better able to aid the befuddled Pickens; two of whom, despite their opposing views, he held in high esteem.

Making things worse was the special bond between Pickens and Bennett. A bond began when the elder politician had been Pickens' mentor as the young, inexperienced legislator groped his way through their state's political maze. It was a friendship that blossomed and later served them both when Pickens came to Washington and needed the influence Bennett could provide from his eminent position on the Hill. A Washington fixture, with a firm grasp on the system, the senator had proven indispensable as a bulwark against the mounting criticism against the president, particularly among those within his own party. Throughout this first term, it was Bennett's vision and sage advice that had guided him through the obstacles which threatened to unravel his controversial lopsided budget that first year and later on, when his factious health care legislation was on the brink of disintegrating. Since then, it had become *de rigueur* to turn to Bennett when a problem of disproportional dimensions presented itself. For Pickens, it simply made good political sense if he wished to survive and succeed in the Washington jungle.

Then, there was Lucerne, who everyone knew to be of high integrity and superior intellect and who lived by the credo, *It isn't who's right but what's right that counts.* Like Pickens, McCurdy was having difficulty reconciling an opposing position to the Marine's unyielding stance to place the country's interests above his own.

"Yes, sir, they do," McCurdy replied to the back of the president's head. "Bennett has never let us down. Yet, I have a nagging feeling that this time his judgment may be clouded."

He was pleased to see Pickens' head bob in agreement.

"I've thought about that, too, Daren," the president said. "Yet, his logic is appealing."

"You mean, that Hussein should've been deposed a long time ago?"

"Exactly," Pickens asserted. "Instead, he's been busting our balls with impunity which, as you know, hasn't done a helluva lot for my image on the international stage."

McCurdy sidestepped the last remark. "Well, I do like Bennett's idea that it doesn't matter who brings him down. As long as it happens on your watch, you'll get the credit. What makes it more attractive is that if Iran does the deed it won't cost us one American soldier and it'll be linked in the history books to the Pickens' administration."

That last comment caused Pickens to swing around. His legacy had been foremost in his mind lately.

But McCurdy's next comment wiped the smile off his face. "Besides, he added, "we're no longer capable of doing it alone now that we've pared the military down."

Squandering the peace dividend was an issue that had been generating an intense amount of criticism lately for Pickens, but it was one which he deflected with pride.

Looking intently at his aide, he said with a hint of satisfaction, "I don't give a rat's ass what those carping war mongers say. History'll prove me right. America's much better off today because of my foresight and commitment to the common man." He slammed his mug down as he spoke, splashing coffee onto the inlaid leather surface of his desk. He brushed the few drops away with his palm and licked it in one motion while falling into, what McCurdy and the other staffers described as his *down home tongue*.

"When the Russkies went belly up we had an obligation to the people to let them share in the peace dividend. If those right wing, conservative pukes had their way we'd still be forking out billions for weapons systems we can't afford and which we ain't got no more use for than a sack of pig manure. And what fo', I ask? So's we can keep our technological edge? Big fuckin' deal! What good's that do when we have illiterate children growing into illiterate adults?"

McCurdy let out a silent sigh. "I agree a hundred percent, Mr. President. But that isn't the issue right now." He'd heard it all before and wasn't interested in another dose of Pickens philosophizing when there was a real life-and-death problem to deal with. "We got ten kids out there that *can* read who we hafta bring home alive," he reminded the president. "And at least two are missing some fingers." He watched Pickens shudder and continued, "And, if Lucerne is correct, we gotta do it without allowing a major power shift in the gulf."

"Okay. Okay," Pickens said impatiently. He found more comfit in discussing his social programs but obviously this wasn't the time for it. "Run over Lucerne's points again for me."

McCurdy nodded. "It's important," he reminded the president, "to remember the vice president and Hemmings concur with him."

"Thanks for reminding me," he said, sourly.

McCurdy looked at his notes. "First. Lucerne argues that since his days are numbered, Hussein's not worth worrying about. The embargo has severely weakened his military which is further constrained by our forces maintaining the no-fly zone. He points out that though Hussein has a large army, it's real strength is limited to the well-equipped Republican Guards he uses to suppress his people."

"We loosened the lid for `em," he mumbled.

"Excuse me?" McCurdy replied.

"The damn embargo and our aid to Iraq's opposition groups," Pickens said. "We weakened the scumbag and that's why Iran wants to attack. We loosened the lid on the jar for `em."

"That was Lucerne's second point," he said, referring back to his notes. "Iran hasn't been sitting on its duff since their 1989 truce with Iraq. With a stable domestic political environment, they've been exporting their brand of Islam throughout the Middle East and into north Africa while aggressively replacing and modernizing military equipment lost during the ten year war with Iraq." McCurdy gave the president a moment to focus on that point then continued, "Hemmings also asserts Iran has the most powerful navy in the gulf, Mr. President. Which is why Lucerne argues they can't be allowed to pursue regional hegemony. He maintains that it's too dangerous and he predicts that if they succeed in overrunning Iraq, their next move will be against Saudi Arabia, which controls sixty percent of the world's known oil supplies."

Once again, Pickens found himself railing against Lucerne and Hemmings, favoring instead, his friend and mentor. "What about Bennett's points?" he interrupted. "There's a good case there, too."

"No question about it. Your policy of reaching out to all those Fundamentalists from Algeria to southern Lebanon would be thrown into question if we entered into a war with Iran now."

"Exactly! Those two blockheads just don't get it. All they want to do is to kill, kill, kill! Hemmings has been opposed to my policy of global harmony from day one. I can't understand why he doesn't comprehend that we can win the Muslims over once they see we aren't the devil. If we're ever going to eliminate terrorism and violence we need to build bridges. How many times must I tell those bozos that we've got to apply the lessons learned from Carter's flawed policy?"

"You've told them," McCurdy said, not wishing to go down that road again. But it didn't stop Pickens.

"Carter was foolish to pressure the Shah on human rights while allowing him to become isolated and vulnerable. That was shortsighted."

"Shortsighted, indeed," McCurdy agreed, while wishing they could move on.

"The Ayatollah wasn't grateful to us for what we did because we only worked the problem from one side of the street - pushing the Shah without stroking the Ayatollah - but now, we're stroking and it'll work, Daren. I just know it'll work."

McCurdy didn't respond.

"Whatsa matter, Daren? You think we screwed up?"

"I don't know anymore. Like you, I thought we were sending the moderate Fundamentalists the right signal. But after the kidnapping and the murder...," his voice trailed off as he struggled to understand the Middle Eastern mind.

"Don't lose faith, my boy," Pickens said, falling into his preacher role. "This world has been dominated by maniacs since the beginning of this century. Is it any wonder those poor Islamics are reacting violently when violence is all they know. We're on the threshold of a new age, Daren. Authoritarianism, vengeance, terrorism, they're all tools of the past. Revolutions are going to become more peaceful as we transition out of the old world and into the new. If a few of the old guard choose to rely on ancient ways, it's only because they, like other militarists, are mired in the past. We're witnessing the final era of man's violent nature. That's why concentrating on the children is so damn important. They're the future."

"Getting back to the problem at hand," McCurdy said, playing to the president's preference for indecision, "let's stall. Surely, if the Iranians want to invade Iraq and you agree to let them, then what difference does a few more days make? They know we've received their message and are working the problem. They also know that governments don't move quickly. Certainly not within ten days. Besides, we're not obliged to jump just because they said so. We're still the most powerful nation in the world. In the meantime, the Navy's Red Cell has begun searching for the mids. If, by tomorrow, they haven't turned up anything and you've made up your mind, you can send the Iranians a signal. Should you agree with Lucerne, then we tell them no and demand the safe return of the mids, or else."

"Or else, what?" Pickens asked, a little bewildered.

"I don't know but I'm sure Lucerne will have several options for you." To his relief, that seemed to satisfy Pickens. "If, on the other hand, you accept Bennett's advice, we'll pull our forces back." He leaned forward and handed Pickens a sheet of paper. "According to Lucerne, these four ships comprise our naval MidEast Force in which there's also a small contingent of marines. As you can see, they're more of a military presence than a force. You can order them out of the gulf and into the Arabian Sea without weakening our position very much."

"But what about the terrorists that kidnapped the mids and killed that professor?" Pickens asked. "If I accept Bennett's advice, we can't just let them get away with it."

"Of course not. But whether or not we catch them, Iran will deny any connection to them. When we do go public we'll link the kidnappers to the fanatical Egyptian fringe group that attacked the World Trade Center. But, privately, through back channels, you let Iran know that in retaliation for taking the mids we will no longer pressure the Egyptians and Algerians to ease up on the Fundamentalists there. You'll make it clear that they can't conduct terrorist activities in this country without paying a price."

Pickens swung his chair so that he was facing the window again. He bit his lower lip and thought a moment. Then, with less anxiety in his voice, he said, "Okay! Let's wait. As we used to say back home, `An action delayed, is the next best thing to an action taken.'" Then, as McCurdy headed for the door, he called, "You tell Lucerne. I'll take care of Bennett."

* * *

Meanwhile, across the Potomac in Arlington, Trish Mathews opened the door to her apartment to Sampson and immediately regretted not having changed out of her workout suit. Her hair, still damp from her shower, hung unevenly around her shoulders, framing a well-scrubbed, pretty face.

"Please excuse me," she demurred, "I'm running late. I just returned from the gym." Then, turning and heading for the bedroom, she called over her shoulder, "Make yourself comfortable while I finish getting dressed."

Sampson called back that it was he who should apologize for arriving early. Then, hearing the hair dryer he went to her desk, where the dining room table should've been and, moving quickly, flipped through her day calendar. The computer monitor was warm. Which meant she hadn't just returned from the gym. Thinking that she'd been working on the midshipmen story, he found her note pad. The first few pages were the notes from her phone conversation with the terrorist. Having seen the copy she willingly provided to Harding, he skipped down to her account of her meeting with the Bennetts, which pretty much described their anxiety and sorrow. Underlined in the margin was a reminder to interview Professor Nolan's wife and the Lucernes. He also looked through the drawers and waste basket but found nothing of interest.

He looked around the apartment. It was tasteful but sparsely furnished. There were two large, overstuffed chairs, the kind he'd seen in Ikea, an older sofa, probably a hand-me-down, and a couple of end tables. There was also a free-standing oak hat rack with a sweater and ball cap on it. Several framed travel posters on the walls suggested she might be a skier. She owned a small, inexpensive television but it's location, between two well-stocked bookcases, gave the impression she didn't have time for it. Except for journalism school textbooks and several paperback novels from a used book store, the majority of her titles focused on the military. On the coffee table he found an exercise magazine and the latest issue of *The Washingtonian*. With the hair dryer still going he peered into the narrow galley kitchen. At first glance it seemed she might be a gourmet cook. There were cookbooks, two Cusinart appliances, an expensive set of German Wusthof Dreizackwerk knives in a butcher block holder, and on the wall above the stove, four French copper pans, like those found in a William-Sanoma catalogue. While impressive, none of it looked used and he guessed they were probably her share of a short-lived marriage. In the cabinets he found a mixed collection of spices, canned goods and cereals. Nothing out of the ordinary. The refrigerator held assorted bags of raw veggies and fruit, a few doggie bags from local restaurants, a half case of German beer and two bottles of white Italian table wine, one half full. The freezer was bare except for a package of chopped meat, a frozen pizza and a bottle of Absolut lemon flavored vodka.

The hair dryer stopped and he moved to the sofa and began thumbing through a magazine.

"Sorry to keep you waiting," she said poking her head through the partially opened door. "I'll be right out. Put on some music if you like. The CD's in the bookcase, next to the tv."

Her taste in music was more eclectic than her reading. She obviously enjoyed big band and country & western but leaned towards the classics. Sampson selected the *Puccini Weekend* and settled back to the strains of Placido Domingo as Rudolfo in *La Boheme*.

A few moments later, when she returned she wasn't the person who'd greeted him. Her auburn hair was woven into a tight single braid that dissected her broad shoulders. Her makeup was understated but effective. And the blue silk shirt, with the sleeves partially rolled up and open collar was bloused at her narrow waist but not so loose that he missed her ample breasts. She had on jeans that, while not tight, let him know that she was indeed shapely, which he may have missed had she kept on her looser fitting sweat pants. She also wore a stylized western belt with a sterling silver buckle and tip and had spritzed on a subtle but alluring perfume.

"Good selection. You enjoy opera?" she asked, crossing to the chair opposite him.

He nodded. "I was raised on it. How `bout you? You go often?"

"No. Can't afford it nor do I have the time. You?" She kicked off her shoes and crossed her feet beneath her.

"When I can." As a rule, Sampson answered questions with minimum detail, preferring to extract information rather than divulging it.

She became flustered at the momentary silence and rebounded by asking, "How clumsy of me. Would you like something to drink? Beer? Wine?"

"Thanks. A beer would be nice." He smiled and followed her with his gaze as she went to the kitchen. "Any preferences?" she called back.

"I'm easy. But, if I have a choice, imported."

"You're in luck. Bottle or glass?"

"Bottle's fine."

She handed him a cold Heineken and resettled in the same chair, nestling her wine glass between her thighs.

Sampson raised his beer, "I wish we had something pleasant to drink to, Miss Mathews," he said, reminding her of the purpose of his visit. "How about, to the safe and speedy return of our midshipmen?"

The reference to the mids made her straighten. She had momentarily forgotten the purpose of his visit. Raising her glass, she echoed the words but her tone made them sound more like a prayer than a toast. "What a horrible thing to happen," she said, with genuine discomfort.

"I agree, Miss Mathews."

"Please call me Trish."

"Okay. My friends call me Duke." He placed his beer on the table and moved to the CD. "Mind if we turn this off now? There are a lot of questions."

"By all means. It was a nice interlude, though."

"Ditto," he said, sitting down and leaning forward with his elbows on his knees. "As I mentioned over the phone, I'm heading the search and rescue mission and I need every bit of information I can get. Even though I know what you told Admiral Harding it's important that we discuss it again. Okay?"

"Sure," she said. She felt comfortable with him. Perhaps because they were in her apartment or, more likely, because she found him attractive. "That's not a problem. I'm a reporter and I take good notes." She retrieved her note pad. "Fire away."

Sampson was a trained interrogator and hostage negotiator and it was easy for him to set the mood while querying her on every detail of her conversation with the terrorist.

Finally, when he'd extracted as much as she had to offer, he said, "There's one more item. Can you describe your impression of the man? Specifically, what feelings and emotions he may have elicited?"

She wrinkled her nose and thought a moment. "It's funny you should ask, Tom. I really hadn't given that any thought since the call. You know, the kidnapping, the professor's death and the demands..., all of which constituted the gist of the story. Yet," she pursed her lips, "there was a definite reaction." Leaning back, she closed her eyes and reflected a moment. "I got a chill listening to him," she began. "Not when he was telling me about the mids and the demands. He was very business-like then. Very explicit. He spoke slowly and calmly. He was concerned that I got every detail. That I understood it all." Then, stroking her arm, she said, "I know it sounds peculiar, but I had an uneasy feeling that he was playing with me. Playing with me sexually. And now that I think about it," she said, looking intently at Sampson, "sadistically, too. I mean, it wasn't like a male-female thing." She paused, finished her wine and said, "I don't know if I'm making sense. It's the first time I've really thought about it. But he scared me and at the same time, I felt violated. There was a tone that I can't quite describe except to say it was clearly sexual, including the pace of his breathing, which changed noticeably when we talked about how I might benefit from this story."

"What bothered you most?" he asked.

This time she didn't hesitate. "His constant use of my first name. It was as though he was trying to reach through the phone and touch me." The idea made her shudder. "It was really weird," she admitted.

"Anything else?"

She shook her head.

He thanked her for being so candid and she smiled.

"Most importantly," he added, "I'm grateful that you're willing to sit on this story while we conduct our search. It's making the task a lot easier. I promise we won't forget what you're doing for us."

She blushed a little. "You needn't feel that way. As an American, I'm as distressed about this as you. Besides, I know the Bennetts and their son. I'll do whatever I can to help you," she said, touching his hand.

As she walked him to the door, he said, "Oh. One other thing. How would you describe his accent?"

Her face twisted. "Accent? He had no accent. Why would you think he had an accent?"

Chapter Seven

At Mrs. Bennett's urging, Trish spent the better part of the following morning at the senator's home. In a sense, it was a relief for both women to discuss the kidnapping since both were bound not to discuss it with anyone outside the loop. Together, they commiserated about young Russell's safety as they tried imagining the scenario of events that followed his abduction and his current state of mind. Though it had been a tiring and emotional experience, Trish returned to work with a keener appreciation for the suffering of family members during crises. As she drove into the garage, she resolved to include that perspective in her story.

She hadn't been at her desk long when the phone rang. "This is Trish Mathews." Her voice betrayed her waning energy.

"Good afternoon, Trish, baby. You sound tired. Whatsa matter? Not getting enough sleep?" She recognized the voice immediately and bolted upright.

"Who is this?" she said, while punching the caller ID. But it was useless. He'd blocked it again.

"Don't play games, Trish," he warned her. "You know who." Though he spoke slowly and distinctly his voice had a mocking tone that both irritated and frightened her. "We'll have time to play later, darling. But not now."

A chill passed through her and she snapped back, "What do you want?" As she spoke she grabbed a pencil and jotted down the time.

"Did you have a nice visit at the Bennetts?"

"What! Are you following me!?" Her raised voice drew unwanted stares and she instantly cupped the phone and hissed into it, "What the hell're you up to? You sonofbitch."

"Ooooh yeah," he crooned. "I like it when you get angry. I was beginning to think you were a typical, unfeeling reporter. Glad to see you're capable of being aroused."

She took a deep breath and, hoping to convey a composed presence for those still watching, she lowered her voice and said more calmly, "Why are you following me? Am I your next victim?"

"Not to worry, doll face. You're a team player. No, ma'am. We don't want anything happening to you, Trish."

Each mention of her name made her cringe and caused her to move the phone to her other ear in a futile effort to distance herself from him. He was holding the phone to his mouth and his heavy breathing made her feel as if he was beside her.

"I want you to deliver another message to the Superintendent and his band of merry men." He paused a moment. "Are you ready to copy?"

"Yes, I am," she sighed with trepidation.

His tone changed abruptly when he next spoke. Once again, he was pure business.

"History's replete with rulers who tried bucking the system and refused to go along with the powers that be. They always suffered for their inaction. You getting my drift?"

"No, I am not."

He sighed. "We haven't seen any U. S. forces moving out of the gulf yet, which might indicate our demands aren't being taken seriously. We don't want that to happen, now, do we?"

"Look," she pleaded, "I have been in contact with Admiral Harding and he assures me your demands are being considered at the highest levels. There's no reason for you to think otherwise," she said, trying to mollify him.

"Why don't we just make sure of that, sweetpea. Tell the good Superintendent to have his marauders visit the western tip of Trotternish, beneath Duntulm Castle."

Confused, she asked, "Trotterwhat? Where? Where the hell's that?" Then, annoyed, she said, "I can't even spell it."

"Not to worry, gorgeous. Do the best you can. They'll know," came the steely reply.

"Is that the entire message?" she said, hoping to draw him out.

He laughed. "Were you expecting another ring?"

She felt his grin and trembled.

"Nooo. There's been enough bloodshed. Please. No more," she begged.

"You have much to learn, Trish. Bloodshed is intricately woven into the fabric of society. It happens every day around the world. There's no escaping it."

The phone went dead before she could respond.

* * *

Sampson knew precisely where Trotternish was and he reacted immediately when told. Travelling by Concorde, he and Cort arrived at Heathrow where they transferred to a waiting RAF transport that took them as far as Glasgow. There, they boarded an RAF helo for the journey to the northern portion of the Isle of Skye, off Scotland's western coast. Arriving as the sun edged toward the horizon, they set down in a broad grassy field midway between the only structure in sight, the white and black Duntulm Castle Hotel, and the jagged ruins of the Duntulm Castle, perched a quarter mile away at the edge of a crumbling promontory, several hundred feet above the turbulent sea. With the aid of the local constabulary, whose headlights illuminated their path, the two SEALs and their British escort, a Scotland Yard agent who'd accompanied them from Heathrow, descended the craggy, weather-worn slopes to the bay. The wind from the sea peppered them with an icy mist while sending waves crashing below them. The steep trail, while well-defined, was wet and dangerous and they moved cautiously. Zigzagging downward, they reached the beach and then followed the narrow shoreline to where the cliffs jutted out abruptly above them. Unable to proceed farther, they climbed the moss laden remains of the ancient castle's defenses that centuries ago had slipped from their moorings into the frosty waters. The rocks were smooth and slick, forcing them to go slowly. As it turned out, they didn't have far to climb. Sampson saw it first, in the beam from Cort's flashlight as it bounced among the rocks and boulders above him. Wedged between two stone slabs, approximately forty feet up the face of the cliff was the cold, stiff body clothed in the uniform the mid had been wearing when abducted. The legs and feet were bound with wire and the hands were stuffed down into the trousers, secured firmly by a knotted rope around the mid's waist. Stabilizing his foothold, Sampson reached in and gently rolled the body toward him. Taking Cort's light, he shone it into the blue, lifeless face and immediately recognized the mid from the personnel files he'd studied earlier. The youngster's name tag, sewn into the shirt above the left pocket, had been removed and in the pocket he saw the remnant of a torn piece of parachute silk.

He turned back to Cort, and with the sea whipping at their feet, he shouted grimly, "Somebody's fucking with us."

Saturday

Chapter Eight

Pickens' spirits and demeanor reflected the cold, gray landscape outside his office. For the past quarter hour he had been pacing beside his desk wishing the approaching meeting away. It was a confrontation he wanted desperately to avoid. But everyone had insisted. To keep it short, he scheduled it in the Oval Office rather than the NSC conference room and made sure only the key players attended. Now, minutes before four, he picked up his mug, took a long sip and stared moodily out at the immutable Washington Monument. News of the midshipman's death had shaken him and added unwanted pressure. Now, he was resentful of anyone with an opinion to offer, including Bennett and his pitiful wife, who had come to see him earlier. Reflecting on their encounter, he cursed them for subjecting him to their wailing protests.

"You've got to do as they say, Les," the midshipman's mother had begged from her chair in the president's private quarters. "We have only the one child," she sobbed. "We can't lose him."

Her drawn, tear-streaked face and red eyes unnerved him and he kept turning away as she urged him to follow her husband's advice.

"Fran, darlin'," he had replied, penitently, "it's not that simple. Believe me, if it were I'd be the first to agree. But...," his voice trailed off as he looked to Bennett for support, while imploring, "Please, Russ. You explain."

The senator, who was as distraught as his wife but more composed, replied, "I can't, Les. Not this time. I don't buy it. I've told you from the beginning how to handle this." There was more than a touch of irritation in his parched voice. "Those sonsofbitches are fucking with you, Les. They're playing you like a fiddle. But, like I said before, there's a way out. Let them have Iraq and that madman Hussein and you'll come out of this smelling like a rose. You've *got* to stop stalling and get on with it," he counseled.

"But the signals are all crossed," Pickens countered.

Bennett looked at him with concern. The president had physically deteriorated since Thanksgiving and his reasoning seemed muddled. "Les...," he began, calmer now.

But Pickens continued, his voice rising. "Every communique we've sent comes back negative. The Iranian party line is the same all over the world. Their ambassador at the UN emphatically denies the kidnapping. The Ayatollah has told our intermediaries in Tehran, the Swiss, the same thing. Russ, they disavow any knowledge of the mids or participating in their abduction." His left eye twitched as he spoke. "They accuse us of concocting the mid story to justify interfering with their plans. Damn it. I feel like I'm being gang raped in a dark alley. I know what they're doing to me, but I don't know who the hell they are." He saw Frances shudder and he said, "I'm sorry, darlin'. That wasn't called for. I apologize."

"Well, you're going to have to do something," Bennett retorted. "You've got my son's life in your hands and if anything happens to him, so help me, I'll use every ounce of energy to bring you down. You payin' attention to me, Les? That's no hollow threat. You'll be dog meat when I'm finished."

"Now, now, Russ. Let's not say things we don't mean." Pickens came across the room and reached out to his friend.

"Cut the crap," Bennett bellowed while pushing the president's hand away. "Don't give me that good-old-boy bullshit. We've known each other too long for that. I'm talking seriously now. If my son goes down, so do you."

Hearing her husband say the words she feared most caused Frances to resume sobbing, making both men shudder.

In the end, it had been a torturous session. Now, alone in the Oval Office, he couldn't shake Bennett's threats. It was the gentle rapping and the door opening that brought him back to the present. Looking up, he saw McCurdy's friendly face and he offered a weak smile.

"Everyone's here, sir," the faithful aide notified him in a soft, reassuring tone. It troubled him that Pickens looked so impotent and beaten so early in the game, and he asked, with obvious concern, "Are you alright, sir?"

For a moment the president seemed not to hear. But then, taking a deep breath and forcing his shoulders back, he nodded and said, "Show them in, Daren."

No one spoke as the handful of men filed in and moved to the chairs arranged around the president's desk.

He waited until they were all seated. Then, licking his lips, he said, referring to the dead midshipman, "Well, it looks like they mean business."

Lucerne wondered mournfully, why it had taken him this long to arrive at that conclusion.

Then, before anyone could respond, the president said, "I've decided to move our forces out of the gulf."

That was the NSC Director's cue to jump in and defuse the opposition by offering his support. "A good decision, Mr. President," Diamond said.

Lucerne wasn't surprised. He had anticipated Bennett's influence on Pickens but he wasn't giving up without a fight. Speaking forcefully, he said, "I must disagree with that position, Mr. President. It is not in our national interests." And then, as Pickens' jaw tightened, he added, "And I urge you to reconsider."

Earlier, he had convinced Gartland, the Secretary of Defense, to delay the Kitty Hawk Battle Group's departure from the Indian Ocean. The nine ship task force had been sailing for Singapore on its way back to the western Pacific after completing a scheduled forty-five day deployment just two days prior to the kidnapping. With Gartland's approval he had instructed the fleet commander to re-direct the ships to the tiny, British naval base on the island of Diego Garcia, in the central Indian Ocean. Technically, the potent force of strike aircraft, Aegis cruisers and modern Arleigh Burke destroyers, with their deadly, long range sub-sonic Tomahawk cruise missiles, were out of the disputed region. But that could change with a little notice. And, even if they didn't attack they were still a bargaining chip to prevent Iran from carrying out its war plans.

"I know your position, general." Pickens said, stiffly, "but, I'm going forward as stated."

"You're making a serious mistake, Mr. President," Lucerne argued. "Iran will walk all over Iraq and they won't stop until they secure Saudi Arabia. Once they set their war machine in motion there'll be no stopping them. They'll assert that any introduction of American forces into the region after they invade is tantamount to an act of war, which will give them an excuse to extend their offensive into the other Arab states. That, then, will signal their Fundamentalist brothers as far away as Morocco and Algiers to rise up in sympathy. In very short order, we'll have a global religious war on our hands. Trying to stop it at that point will be like stamping out a forest fire with your boot - an impossibility! You'll be playing right into their hands."

"And the mids? What about the mids?" Pickens retorted, his voice cracking. "One is already dead. How many more must die? Are we simply to forget about them?" Instantly, he regretted his words as he caught a momentary pained expression in Lucerne's eyes.

There was an awkward silence as the others watched Lucerne exert his will over the president.

"There are times," he responded, solemnly, "when we must put the country above individuals. I believe this is such a time."

Pickens reached for his mug and took a long drink before responding.

"Thank you for the civics lesson, general, but you needn't remind me of what's best for America." He then straightened his bulk, trying without success to appear larger than his opponent across from him. "I have taken an oath to uphold the constitution, which includes safeguarding the country. I don't share your assessment of the Iranian threat. I believe they are simply redressing a wrong that is founded in a long history of turmoil in that region. Must I remind you that the two nations are historical enemies and nothing we can do will change that? Fortunately for us," he added, with a smile, "that enmity will now work to our advantage as one of our foes eliminates the other. Certainly, you'll agree *that's* in our best interests."

Lucerne leapt at the challenge. "No, sir. I don't. Letting Iran out of the cage is a big mistake. Right now, we've got Saddam contained. But if we let Iran attack we'll wind up with a disintegrated and fragmented Iraq, with as few as twenty and as many as sixty groups vying for power. The last thing we need in that region is another rogue state. It'll be disastrous."

Pickens had already made up his mind. He shook his head and said, "I am ordering a withdrawal of our naval surface forces from the gulf immediately." Turning to the Deputy Secretary of State, he directed, "I want you to convey to the Iranian UN delegation that we are doing so and will hold them personally responsible for the safety of our midshipmen."

Lucerne and Hemmings exchanged glances.

Afterwards, as they left the Oval Office, Lucerne told Hemmings of his plan to hold the Kitty Hawk battle group in the Indian Ocean.

"How far are you planning to move the contingent in the gulf?" he asked.

"You heard the president," Lucerne said with a wink. "We'll move the surface forces out over the horizon immediately."

"Wait a minute. What about the submarine?"

"I didn't hear him mention anything about a submarine."

Hemmings smiled. "You sly devil."

"Don't tell me you wouldn't be doing the same thing."

"With this dolt I'd always be watching my sixes," he said, referring to Pickens. "You'd be a fool not to leave yourself some wiggle room - just as you're doing with the battle group. You're lucky to have Gartland as SecDef. He'll support you one hundred percent."

"Yeah," Lucerne said with a heavy sigh. "God works his small miracles." Then, he said, "I've already moved the SEALs from the flagship to the sub and transferred it to CentCom."

"Good move. That'll put her directly under your command."

"And I'm keeping her there."

"Another sound decision. Which one've you got?"

"One of life's ironies. It's the ANNAPOLIS."

"Sounds like God wears dress blues," Hemmings said with a smile. "You gathering the target data from the satellites?"

"Already done. Its being converted, as we speak."

The two men walked past the Marine sentry on their way back to the tunnel.

"Good afternoon, Marine," they said in unison.

He saluted smartly and replied, "Good afternoon, gentlemen."

* * *

"I'm having difficulty accepting your premise, Tom," Harding told Sampson soon after the SEAL's return from Scotland.

The two were sequestered in the admiral's quarters, a large, decorous residence between the stately campus chapel and Bancroft Hall. They sat in the paneled third floor room that served as a private study. It had originally been one of the servant's quarters, when the superintendent was entitled to them decades ago. But that had changed and the small room was eventually converted to its current role.

"I understand, admiral. But it adds up." He insisted. "There are too many clues."

"Clues? Don't you mean evidence?"

"No. I mean clues."

Harding gave him a measured look. "I've always thought of you as logical and levelheaded. *Clues* implies the kidnappers are purposely leaving a trail. That they *want* to be found. That makes no sense, Tom."

Sampson could see where Harding was going with this; that this was too serious an op to jeopardize on half-assed theories and if he pressed too hard he might be reassigned. But he was adamant. "Hear me out," he countered. "First, the mids didn't have to be kidnapped for the Iranians to make war on Iraq. Between Africa, North Korea and Bosnia, our forces are spread so thin we couldn't possibly respond as we did in ninety-one and they know that. So, why do it? I think they're using it to twist the knife. They waited until the chairman was hospitalized so they could take the children of two people with direct access to Pickens during this crisis."

Harding nodded. He and Hemmings had had this same discussion. "But how's that connect with your suspicion about the clues?"

"I was getting to it. Iran can carry out terrorism with the best of them but I think this op goes beyond their capabilities. I'm sure they're behind it," he admitted. "And no doubt they're financing it, too. But they didn't run it. I'm convinced they brought somebody else aboard to plan and carry it out."

Harding respected Sampson and though he was skeptical, he listened.

"Whoever did it couldn't have acquired all the necessary intel in the brief time since the JCS announcement of the chairman's prostate operation - and that's when I figure they started putting their plan together. With that short fuse they needed somebody with more than a basic knowledge of the school to conduct the surveillance phase. If it was me, once I decided on my targets, I'd be a frequent visitor here. I'd move around the yard as if I belonged, learning the daily routines of my targets, their class schedules as well as the faculty's and brigade's movements. I'd also monitor the evening muster procedures and the guards' and duty officers' routines. Obviously, that's what they did. And, they did it with a minimum of intel collectors and without drawing attention to themselves. If they were Iranians you would've known it."

"So you think they hired somebody, an American, possibly a former Navy man?"

"More than just a former Navy man."

Harding wasn't convinced.

Sampson pulled out the piece of torn parachute silk from his pocket. "I found it in the dead mid's pocket. It was put there to be found."

"What is it?" he asked as he examined the handkerchief-size cloth.

"It's a piece of parachute cloth and it was used to kill the mid," he replied with conviction.

"I thought he drowned."

"He did. But not in any body of water. He was dead long before we got to him. I'm sure the autopsy will show he was murdered within twenty-four hours of being kidnapped and his body put there at least a day before we were alerted."

Harding shook his head. "That doesn't track, Tom. He was killed because the president hadn't moved fast enough," he said, repeating what the terrorist had told the newswoman. Harding was a warrior but he'd never operated in this environment and he was having difficulty accepting Sampson's reasoning.

"I don't believe that. It was a convenient excuse but I'm sure his death had nothing to do with prodding the president. I'll bet they would've given us another reason had Pickens reacted immediately to their demands."

Harding rubbed his eyes. He was tired. "Are you saying the kidnapper has his own agenda, one that isn't part of Iran's invasion plan? That nothing the president does will prevent him from killing our kids?"

"Nothing short of tracking the fucker down and killing him first," the SEAL replied, coldly. "He's playing with us, admiral, just like Iran is playing with Pickens. Our boy died a cruel death and I'm sure it was done for two reasons. One was to intimidate the other mids and keep them in line. Dying like that is brutal," he explained. "Watching someone die like that is a close second. The other reason was to send us a signal."

Harding didn't want to know but he asked. "How did he die?"

"We call it drown proofing. It's a field interrogation technique we used frequently in Nam. It's very effective. You can use a silk scarf or nylon stocking but parachute silk was the handiest. We tied our man down, usually in front of his comrades, placed the cloth over his face and then poured a little water on it. The water closes the pores allowing him to breathe out but not in. It's a long and tortuous procedure in which the victim gets only water when he inhales. If he doesn't talk he drowns in eight ounces of water."

Harding stiffened, "Those bastards did that to our mid?"

"I'm sure of it. And, furthermore, they want us to know it. That's why they left the cloth behind. And," he said, with confidence, "that's why I don't think we're dealing with Iranians. That isn't one of their techniques. The dismembered fingers, yes. But, not this."

Harding stroked the cloth with his large hands as if it were a sacred relic. Then, after a moment, he asked in a flat tone, "You know, don't you? You know who they hired."

"Not specifically. If you don't mind, I'd like to hold on to this," he said, retrieving the cloth and folding it carefully. As he returned it to his pocket, he dropped the bombshell. "You're not going to like it. They bought one of our guys."

"Jesus Christ, Tom! How the hell did you make that leap!? There are plenty of specialists out there with your killing skills..., Germans, Brits, Israelis, even the IRA. Any one of whom could do the recon here in the yard without being noticed. Why in god's name recruit a SEAL? And, more importantly, where would they find somebody who'd turn on his country like that? Sign up with fanatics against his own shipmates? No. I can't believe..., I won't believe anyone in the program would buy into that. It's preposterous."

It was a natural reaction and Sampson said, "I felt the same way, admiral. But then something changed my mind."

"For god's sake, what?" he barked. He wasn't taking this well.

"You know we travel the globe - training in deserts, jungles, mountains. The whole nine yards."

Harding offered a weary nod, he was working to keep his mind open.

"Those cliffs where we found our mid, sir, I know them well. They're the same cliffs Red Cell has used to train. Been there many times."

Harding's gaze widened. But it was what Sampson said next that removed any doubts.

"When Trish Mathews asked the caller to be more specific about the site, he told her not to worry and he assured her, I'd know the precise location."

Harding slumped back. "What do we do now?"

Chapter Nine

The mids were being held together in one large room of a damp basement. Three-foot lengths of chain secured to each mid's ankle ran to rings set deep in the concrete floor. They could stand but were tethered far enough apart to prevent them from reaching out and touching one another. They had been there since their abduction, usually sitting with their backs to the wall facing the center of the large open room. A coarse wool blanket and a honey bucket, retrieved and taken to the bathroom each morning, were their only accommodations.

As a rule, they were left unattended but they never knew when the heavy door would open and their captors would enter. The routine was anything but routine. Even their meals were given without a set pattern. Of necessity, conversations were stilted and infrequent. Left to their own devices, they were quick to fashion a covert means of communicating. From the outset Ingrid assumed the mantle of leadership. As the hours extended into days, ignoring her injury, she rallied them to keep their spirits up and insisted they accompany her in a daily exercise regimen. Her strength of character and her refusal to bend to her captors' will held them together whenever morale began flagging. Rebellious by nature, she flaunted the rules, particularly the one not to speak, and kept reminding her classmates of their obligation to escape.

Late one evening, straining against her bindings, she leaned forward and whispered across the room to Bennett. "Psst. Russ. How's it going? You haven't said much lately. You wanna talk?"

Bennett had become morose and would've been content to remain withdrawn had she not kept after him. This time he stirred but didn't reply. When she called out again he responded by wrapping his blanket tighter around him.

"Damn it, Russ. Snap out of it!" she commanded. "We can't let the bastards win. Now, tell me. How're you feeling? I'm talking to you, Russ."

She wouldn't be put off. Persisting, she kept it up until he raised his head. Reluctantly, he offered her a weak smile then rolled over toward the wall.

Like the others, his morale had fallen dramatically after being forced to watch Valerius' torturous death. Unschooled in terrorist tactics, they had no idea Valerius had been selected because he was the strongest and most physically fit among them. Taking him out made the others feel vulnerable and impotent and thus, easier to control. Likewise, the sexual assault of the other female, the weakest of the group, further eroded their spirits.

The girl, a slight, fair-skinned beauty, had begun sobbing uncontrollably soon after the assault on Valerius, particularly whenever the guards entered. Conscious of her role, Ingrid was making headway by reassuring her they would be rescued while also encouraging her to be brave. Then, late one night after dinner, the guards came and unshackled her while the others looked on helplessly. Ignoring Ingrid's shouts to return her, they took the frightened girl to an adjoining room. There, she was raped, first by the leader and then by several of his comrades while he video taped the ordeal with morbid fascination. The walls were thick but not so thick as to prevent the mids from hearing her screams. Straining at her shackles, Ingrid responded by shouting obscenities through the wall at them, calling them depraved, gutless cowards while her classmates listened in shocked silence to the girl's pained screams. After a while there was silence and Ingrid and the others feared the worst. Finally, after nearly an hour, the girl was returned battered and dazed. They had obviously gone beyond rape. Her open shirt revealed garish bruises across her bare chest. Her once-pretty features were now grotesquely distorted - lips and nose bloody and swollen, eyes puffy and closed. Two men carried her in as if she were a sack of trash and re-attached her leg chain, leaving her in a heap with her underpants and trousers hanging loosely around her knees. The dim ceiling light above her revealed patches of blood in her matted hair. Unable to reach and comfort her, the others whispered encouragement and prayers that seemed not to register. She lay there for a long while before stirring. Then, moving slowly and with great pain, she tugged at her clothes until she covered herself. Those closest to her tossed their blankets over her but she seemed not to notice. Throughout the night she would let out occasional moans but otherwise lay still. In the morning, when the guards entered with food she wrapped the blankets around herself and retreated against the wall. When they approached her, she covered her chest with her arms and emitted a series of animal-like groans. When the guards had left Ingrid tried coaxing her friend back to the present while vowing vengeance.

With morale at its lowest, Ingrid began relating war stories told to her by her father. Tales of gallant Marines, who, against overwhelming odds, had survived and lived to tell about it. Like a missionary, she was relentless in sustaining their morale and insisting that everyone remain tuned in to their captors' routine for any clue that might offer an opportunity for escape. She even established a duty roster that ensured someone was always awake to listen for any sound from outside their cell. Soon, they could tell by the shuffle of footsteps from the floor above when the leader returned, an event that usually brought out many of his men. Intrigued by his demeanor, Ingrid had been watching him since realizing the anti-terrorist exercise had been a ruse. She had noted his domineering personality and hyperbolic mood swings with interest. But what intrigued her most was his peculiar style of leadership; one that centered on macho bonding that included an extraordinary amount of physical contact with his men, like throwing powerful punches and encouraging them to do the same. Likewise, he would grab them and wrestle them to the ground. She guessed he got away with it because he wasn't malicious and, too, because of his disarming manner. While not the biggest of his men, he was powerful and seemed to have an enormous reservoir of energy. As the undisputed leader, he would move among his clique sustaining an ongoing banter in a clipped speech pattern that she found difficult to decipher. It all made her wonder with amusement if perhaps he was a latent homosexual.

What unnerved her most was his penetrating stare and those instances when he seemed to be looking through or beyond the mids. On those occasions she feared their fate had been decided and she prayed for an early rescue.

Now, listening while the others slept, she discerned heavy footsteps, first above her and then in the hallway outside. From the sound of the muffled voices, there were several men and she tensed when they stopped outside the door. A moment later the bolt slid back and the heavy door slammed against the wall. The crash, which was meant to frighten them, did just that. It was the leader. Unlike the others, who came and left with military efficiency, he enjoyed more dramatic entrances. This time, under the fixed stares of his captives and his men, who remained in the doorway, he strode across the room and stood above Ingrid. Having identified her early on as their leader it evolved that he would address only her. Tonight he was wearing a black pullover, tight jeans and polished Wellingtons and smelled of alcohol and cheap cologne. Despite his menacing look she made no attempt to stand or move, but remained seated with her back to the wall and her legs stretched out between his feet. Refusing to be intimidated, she looked up with icy contempt, ignoring the beam from his flashlight that he played onto her groin and then up to her breasts. He stood silent for a long while offering only a thin smile across his bearded face and she wondered with growing concern if this was the prelude to another sexual assault.

Finally, he said, "How're we holding up, pussycat? You're hand feeling better?" The words were soft but mocking. "You ready to play?" he cooed. With that, he produced a square of parachute silk and brushed it across her face.

She didn't think he meant it but remained silent to avoid provoking him into harming one of the others.

"How 'bout a fuck, pussycat? Just you and me. One on one. No rough stuff. Ya interested?" He clicked his tongue in a crude, suggestive manner. And when she failed to respond he leaned down and cupped her breasts. "Oooo," he said to the amusement of his men, who were now hooting their encouragement. "That's nice, baby."

Ingrid remained stone still, making no attempt to disguise the scorn she felt for him. Unconcerned, he squeezed until she winced.

Then clamping his beefy hand over her chin, he pulled her face to his and whispered, "Thought you'd like to know we're making progress, princess. I expect you'll be seeing some heavy duty fireworks soon."

He could see she didn't understand and he said, "We're gonna even the score with some old shipmates, darlin'. Like they say in the Navy, `Paybacks are hell.' And, if you ain't already figured it out, pussycat, you're the bait."

She tried turning her head away but he held her and pushed his thumb against her lips, forcing them into a distorted half smile. Sensing he was aroused, she shoved him but it was like pushing a wall. Amused, he grabbed a knot of her hair and jerked her head back. Then, pressing his flashlight up between her legs, he forced her back against the wall so that her leg was stretched by the chain. Now, with nowhere to move, she slammed her fists into his ribs and immediately recoiled at the searing pain.

"Hey! We got ourselves a real tiger," he said with a toothy grin.

Incensed, she swung again, using only her good hand this time. But it was more symbolic than effective. He was solid muscle and she had no room to put anything behind her punch.

"I think she likes me," he called to his troops, who indicated their approval with a series of grunts.

Before she could strike again he was smothering her with his hairy face and forcing his thick tongue into her mouth. She pushed and twisted but it was useless. Breathing through flared nostrils, he held the kiss which kept her from breathing. She tried bringing her knee up but there was no play in the chain. Finally, when it seemed her lungs would burst he released her and she leaned forward, gasping. Repulsed by the act and the aftertaste of chewing tobacco and alcohol, she gagged then spit blindly, not caring that she'd soiled his shoes.

* * *

Meanwhile, in Annapolis, everything was supporting Sampson's initial belief that the mids hadn't left the area by sea. Further, if they were still in the country, as he suspected, it made sense that they were nearby.

From the Coast Guard, McLeod had learned that the busy port of Baltimore had experienced an unusual downturn during Thanksgiving. Of the eight merchant ships in port, all had arrived before the kidnapping and none had departed since. To be certain the mids weren't aboard any of them a contingent of SEALs searched each of them. As a further precaution, working with the Coast Guard, Red Cell also checked marinas as far south as Norfolk. Again, they found no clues suggesting any had been used as a staging area to transfer the hostages or to refuel the abductor's boat. Everything seemed to indicate the boat escape was a diversion aimed at delaying the Navy's progress.

"The way I see it," Sampson told the FBI agent, "the terrorists need a hideout large enough to accommodate ten mids." He paused, and corrected himself, "...nine mids, their guards and gatekeepers."

"What's your best guess on the size of their team?" Cutler asked.

Sampson had already done the calculations. "By their own admission they intend holding the mids for at least ten days. That'll require a bigger force than if they held them two or three days. Keeping prisoners under twenty-four hour surveillance, they're going to need a minimum of one guard standing a two hour shift every eight hours. That'll give `em time to eat, sleep and do other duties. Right there, you're looking at a minimum of four men. Then, they'll need perimeter guards. Depending on how large an area, the terrain, how sophisticated their comms are..., you gotta figure all together maybe twenty to thirty."

"Sounds like a small army," the agent said.

"It gets more complicated," McLeod chimed in. "They're going to need a place to house and feed them. And if they're the pros we think they are, they'll billet them away from the mids. Things can get messy if you keep everyone under the same roof," he explained. "Then there's the matter of transportation." McLeod paused and spit his tobacco juice into a stained styrofoam cup. "They probably have a combination of vans and cars - nothing that would draw attention to them but still a significant number. And, they'll want to keep them out of view. For that, they'll need at least one large building or several small ones."

"Unless," Cutler said confidently, "they're using a safe house in the inner city. Then the vehicles will blend with the rest of the urban traffic. As far as storing them, there's always public garages. They'd certainly blend in there. Right?"

Sampson nodded. "You may have something there. But I'm inclined to think otherwise."

"Whatdya mean?" Cutler sounded disappointed.

Sampson moved across the office to a map of the mid-Atlantic that he'd taped to the wall and on which he'd placed a series of concentric circles emanating out from Annapolis.

"Assuming they made their escape over land, they had to get to wherever they were going ASAP. You know, minimize their time on the road before the mids are discovered missing at evening muster. Now," he said, tracing one of the outer circles with his finger, "this is about as far as you can drive in four hours if you hold to the speed limit. And since they couldn't afford to be stopped, I'm guessing that's what they did. How many large cities within this area?" he asked the agent.

"Well...," Cutler said while studying the map, "you got Richmond, the District, Baltimore, Willmington and Philly, if you push it."

"You get a gold star. As you can see, there aren't many options if you want a city to hide in."

"All you need is one," the agent replied.

Sampson shook his head. "I don't believe they would chance it. Too many eyes."

"Well, you minimize that by finding a safe house somewhere in suburbia," the agent countered. "Look at this region," he said, indicating the area between Baltimore and Washington. "It's all suburbs. The same's true north and west of Baltimore and, likewise for the District and northern Virginia. They got a lot of choices."

"No," Sampson said, shaking his head. He'd thought it all out before. "That wouldn't work. They'd be noticed because folks notice strangers in their neighborhoods."

"Well," Cutler said, "using your logic, that about kills your theory that they're in the area. If they aren't at sea, or in another country, or the cities or suburbs, what's left?"

"If he's one of us, then he's gone to where SEALs feel comfortable."

"What the hell does that mean?   Under the sea?" Cutler quipped.

"I think he's somewhere out here," Sampson said, indicating a large unpopulated area of the map. "Somewhere in the wild."

Cutler studied the map. "Well, he better be careful. We're in the middle of deer season, you know."

Chapter Ten

Having completed its transit through the Gulf of Oman the Japanese freighter, Nisho Maru, prepared to alter course westward toward Bahrain on the final leg of its long journey. Out on the starboard wing of the bridge the navigator noted the sequence of bearings taken from the massive radar antennae at Bandar Abbas, Iran's Persian Gulf naval base, and entered them into his log. His next task would be to plot the ship's position on the chart and then recommend a course change to the captain. It was a routine procedure, one the veteran seaman had performed hundreds of times without incident. However, on this sunny but hazy day, as he returned to the chart house there was a muffled explosion aft, toward the stern. In the next instant a plume of water rose up and the ship shuddered violently, causing him to lose his footing. Instinctively, he reached for the steel door handle several inches away but missed it. As alarms went off and the crew scrambled to their stations he was hurled backwards against the iron stanchion supporting the compass. With everyone's attention directed toward the stern it would be a while before anyone noticed his lifeless body at the base of the metal post, blood oozing from his ears and nose.

Unlike the unsuspecting Nisho Maru, the government in Tehran anticipated the disaster. Soon after the explosion it reacted quickly by issuing a notice to mariners alerting them to the mines, while also claiming they had been sown by Iraq during the Persian Gulf war and were now loose and drifting toward the narrow and heavily traversed Hormuz Strait. The notice automatically triggered an aspect of international maritime regulations that absolved insurance companies from paying reparations to ship owners operating in the area in disregard of the warning. The net effect was that vital shipping traffic came to a temporary standstill until the area could be swept and declared safe, a task that fell to Iran's small mine sweeping force.

* * *

Until that moment Lucerne's warnings to Pickens, that he suspected Iranian gun boats operating in the channel of laying mines, had been greeted with little enthusiasm. Now, in the wake of the Nisho Maru incident and an outcry from the international community, the president promptly modified his earlier decision by accepting Lucerne's recommendation to relocate Italian-based American F-16 squadrons to eastern Turkey and deploy the aircraft carrier Saratoga, now moored in Sicily's Augusta Bay, to the eastern Mediterranean. At least, Lucerne thought, he hasn't completely lost touch with reality. Yet, with the crisis gaining momentum, he was increasingly troubled by the president's odd behavior, particularly as conveyed to him earlier by Diamond, the NSC Advisor, who rarely criticized Pickens.

"McCurdy told me," he had whispered to Lucerne in a private meeting between the two men, "that Pickens is complaining that everyone thinks he's so strong when sometimes it's all he can do to get through the day. Frankly, I'm worried. He doesn't look at all well. And with regard to this problem, McCurdy says he's doing whatever he can to avoid it. He says Pickens hardly sleeps. He's up all hours watching movies or studying issue books and then calling staff officers responsible for the books at home to discuss them." They had been alone in Diamond's office, with no one around to hear them. Clearly, this couldn't be repeated. "He's consuming enough food for ten men," Diamond went on. "The chef has had to keep the kitchen manned around the clock. I've never seen such compulsive behavior."

Lucerne was sympathetic. Yet, as one of a handful of officials privileged to see the CIA's psychological profile of the president, he understood what was happening. The detailed report - highlighting his roots in an alcoholic family - had been prepared when Pickens became a serious contender in the presidential campaign. Tracing his behavior throughout his adolescent and adult years, the agency's psychologists had categorized him as a latent dysfunctional, who could slip over the edge during periods of excessive pressure.

Now, in Hemmings' office, having shared Diamond's observations to the CIA Director, Lucerne added his own concerns. "You've read his profile. This situation with Iran duplicates the pressures he experienced from his alcoholic father."

"You think they've done the same analysis?" the director asked.

"Of course we can't be sure. But clearly they're creating a significant amount of tension and dissonance in his life."

"Be specific," Hemmings said while extending one of two cigars to his friend.

Lucerne declined with a wave. "I've been talking with Captain Joe Ward, one of the Navy's pioneers in the treatment of substance abuse. He's out of the service now and on the staff at the Betty Ford Foundation, where they've been studying the effects of alcoholism on family members. They've concluded that dependents of alcoholics must be viewed as a separate entity and given their own special treatment. According to Ward, that's the only way of preventing kids from growing into dysfunctional adults like our boy, Pickens."

Hemmings pondered the notion from beneath a cloud of smoke. "If Iran's figured this out they're doing a helluva job on him."

Lucerne nodded. "Ward says that communications in alcoholic families takes the form of a triangle, with the child acting as messenger between his frustrated and angry parents. Neither one wants to address the problems associated with drinking so they use the innocent kid as a go-between. Imagine his confusion and pain as he conveys one parent's disapproval to the other one."

"So," Hemmings interjected, "the enemy kidnaps and tortures our mids, even kills one. Then, when pressed through diplomatic channels, denies it completely while sending conflicting demands via third parties, like that reporter at the *Post*. Sounds too sophisticated for them."

"I had the same reaction," Lucerne conceded. "But, considering the stakes, don't you agree it would be foolish to dismiss the theory? Ward maintains, that when innocent people - in this instance, the mids - are victimized because one of the participants in the triangle is unable to confront and solve the problem directly, that scenario resurrects his childhood experiences. At that point his inner pain, which becomes unbearable, throws him into a dysfunctional mode that's manifested by severe depression, helplessness, hopelessness and compulsiveness."

"That pretty much describes our boy," Hemmings admitted. "I guess when you toss someone of Bennett's stature into the equation, his world starts looking pretty damn frenetic."

"Poor bastard," Lucerne added somberly. "And to complicate matters, Bennett's extended a carrot by convincing our young leader that allowing Iran to overthrow the evil Hussein will win him back the voters' hearts in his bid for a second term."

"If Ward's assessment is accurate, it wouldn't be wise to inform Pickens about our submarine," Hemmings said. "We wouldn't want to give him more options than he already has with the F-16s and the Saratoga. There's no telling what he might do."

"I agree. It serves no purpose. Besides, it's a benign force at the moment. More importantly, god knows what he'd have us do."

"Yeah," Hemmings said with a crooked smile, "He might order the skipper to scuttle it as a good will gesture."

"Don't laugh," Lucerne countered. "The man's becoming dangerous. Anything's possible."

"Speaking of the sub, how's it doing?" the director inquired. "I'm sure Iran's already deployed their Kilos," he said, referring to the two Russian-built, diesel submarines they purchased in 1992 and 1993.

"She's doing fine. The Kilos were moved last week from Bandar Abbas out of the gulf to Chah Bahar. We thought at the time it was for training. It's obvious now, they intend using them to prevent forces from going in to clear the mines."

Both men were familiar with Iran's order of battle.

"It was a smart move," Hemmings conceded. "Their role in the gulf is limited and they would've been sitting ducks alongside the pier. They're of more use to Iran in the Arabian Sea. What about their surface force?"

"All in the gulf. Looks like they're throwing everything they have into this one - a classic blitzkrieg op," Lucerne predicted.

"Who's our sub skipper?" Hemmings asked.

"Lucerne grinned. "I was waiting for that. You're going to love this one. Commander Dan Cherico!"

"No shit! Steamin' Louie's son?" Hemmings slapped the arm of his chair. "I'll be dipped in shit. You know he was my company commander at the academy? Sonofagun! I haven't thought about Louie for years. He was a great quarterback, you know." Hemmings' expression changed as a flood of memories surged through him and he thought of his long-dead schoolmate.

Lucerne, who had entered the academy ten years after Hemmings, had had to memorize many of the two football stars' game statistics when he was a plebe. Their exploits on and off the field were legendary, the stuff alumni never tired of repeating at reunions. Now, the small silver nameplate in Heroes' Hall along with his athletic trophies in the field house were all that remained of the fiery aviator. Neither his body nor his plane had been recovered from the Laotian jungle, where he had crashed while returning to his carrier after taking out a group of VC that had been holding down an infantry patrol. As the Air Group Commander, Cherico wasn't required to fly combat missions but he'd insisted, refusing to send his pilots off without first knowing what the enemy could throw against them.

Hemmings tucked his recollections into some distant corner and turned to Lucerne, "God, John, it's over thirty years since he went down." He shook his head. "Young Cherico played pretty damn good ball too, as I recall."

"Wide receiver. Scored against Army three out of four years. He's turned out to be a fine officer."

"How do you assess his situation in the gulf?"

"I'm not too concerned," Lucerne said with confidence. "Iran's got a total of eight destroyers, frigates and corvettes. As long as they don't know he's there he can hide behind the noise of other ships, the thermal layers and the coastal distortions."

"And comms?"

"State-of-the-art UHF, EHF, VHF and ELF. Right now, we're communicating through Milstar, downlinking to his periscope-mounted dish. As you know, it's very secure. There's no back scatter from his antenna, which prevents tracing, intercepting or jamming. He's squirting digital data to the satellite on one frequency and pulling stored data down on a second frequency. His comm suite is ideal for this type of situation. He's never exposed for more than a few minutes."

"I suppose," he said wistfully, "if we're going to have anybody in there, Steamin' Louie's boy is as good as anyone." He thought a moment and then added, "I'd hate to think of what might happen if Iran succeeds."

"Simple," Lucerne responded, "we either pay the ransom or go in after the sub."

Hemmings let out a long sigh. "What a hell of a scenario! There's no way Pickens could stand the pressure."

* * *

Melissa Pickens stood behind her husband and pressed her strong fingers deep into his flesh.

"You must relax, dear," she repeated in a soft, comforting tone. "You made the right decision. Look at what Grenada did for Reagan and Panama for Bush."

"I know," he replied. "But, I'm still uncomfortable about moving those forces within striking range. What if it backfires?"

"How can it, sugar? You've complied with their demands by moving our ships out of the gulf. What can possibly go wrong? Les, sweetheart, trust me. You need a nice war. After Iran topples Saddam and we get the mids back, all you need do is move the carrier into the Red Sea and threaten to unleash our forces. You probably won't even have to fire a shot. Just draw a line in the sand, to borrow a phrase. Tell Iran they have twenty-four hours to begin pulling out of Iraq or we'll blow their Arab asses off the face of the earth."

"They're Persians, dear. Not Arabs," he corrected her, gently.

"Whatever."

"I just don't understand how everything turned to crap," he said. "One day we're on top of the world, the new saviors of America. And the next, we're fighting for our political survival. Where did we go wrong, pumpkin?" Pickens pulled the half-empty bowl of pretzels closer.

"It's too late to worry about it, doll face. But I assure you we'll reverse things." Her fingers kneaded deeper as she spoke, unaware of his pained expression. "We've got so much potential, so much to offer this damn country. We'll leave a legacy that'll make your predecessors pale in comparison. We'll lead this lousy country into the new world order and centuries from now, historians will credit us as pioneers. Our names will be synonymous with the new global village."

Her voice grew intense as she dreamed her dreams and pummeled his plump shoulders. She was committed to her ideals and if these pep talks were necessary to boost his sagging ego in order to achieve them, she would be there for him. Melissa Pickens was not one to be denied her place in history. He'd fumbled the presidency badly - worse than anyone could have predicted - now, the task of recovering the ball and winning the game had fallen to her, the one person who knew and understood his weaknesses. They had survived the off-year election without losing many more Congressional seats and state houses. But the sad truth was that the rift in their own party was widening and Melissa had grown frightened at the prospect of becoming an outcast. The notion of having their political careers cut short was paralyzing. She couldn't bear the thought of not enjoying the exalted status of elder stateswoman, which in her mind was America's equivalent to royalty. She had worked hard for it and deserved it.

The moment the Iranian crisis developed she saw it as an opportunity. Had it not been for the unfortunate coincidence that her husband's mentor's son was one of the victims, she would have convinced him early on to strengthen his position in the gulf. Unfortunately, Bennett had prevailed. But now that that setback was resolved, she was feeling more comfortable. A small successful war would turn things around for them and they could refocus their attention on more important global issues. After that, President Pickens would make the inevitable transition to UN Secretary General, the first American president to hold that position. It would be wonderful, she mused. Together, they'd raise the prestige of the UN to new heights!

* * *

Trish stood before her bathroom mirror removing the last of her makeup while softly humming Puccini's La Boheme. She wore only a large, formless t-shirt that fell to her thighs, one of several that she slept in. The mining incident in the gulf was the first public indication that her story was beginning to unfold and she was growing anxious. Lost somewhere between Puccini and the Pulitzer, she was jarred by the disharmonious chirping of the phone in the next room. Tired, and anxious for sleep, she resented the intrusion and decided to let the night clerk in the lobby take the message. But after several persistent rings it was evident he had other plans. It was nearly eleven thirty when she stomped into the living room and picked up the phone.

"Trish here," she said curtly, making no attempt to conceal her annoyance.

"Evening, Trish."

At the sound of his voice she dropped onto the sofa more frightened than annoyed.

"I hate bothering you at home, darlin', especially at this hour." His casual familiarity was laced with sarcasm. "You sound a bit cranky, Trish. Is it that time of the month?" He didn't bother waiting for her response before continuing, "Or, are you getting ready for bed?"

The question startled her and suddenly, looking down at her bare legs, she felt his gaze and she shuddered. The notion that he might actually be spying on her made her check the window. She hadn't closed the curtains and now the security of the ninth floor dissipated as she looked out and saw neighbors who were unaware or unconcerned they could be seen. Several apartments were dark and she imagined he might be calling from one of them. Cradling the phone between her head and shoulder, she pulled her shirt down over her folded legs while leaning over and turning off the lamp.

"How'd you get my number?" she demanded, a little more secure now that the room was dark.

"You'd be surprised how much I know about you, Trish," he chuckled.

Her temper rose and she hurled questions at the faceless intruder, who now seemed to be threatening her own well-ordered, private life.

"Why? I mean, why are you doing this horrible thing? Who the devil are you? Where are you and why are you spying on me?"

"Relax, Trish," he interrupted calmly and without rancor. "You're right to be upset. I'm sorry to bother you this way. Nobody wants to hurt you. Believe me, I wish I didn't have to drag you into this mess."

For the first time he sounded penitent, almost contrite and she felt guilty.

"Regrettably, there will always be innocent bystanders in matters such as this. It's the nature of the game," he told her.

"Game!? You call killing that defenseless midshipman and dumping his body on the Scottish cliffs a *game*?" She felt her anger returning. "I can't buy that line of bullshit, mister. Why'd you kill that boy? How many more are you going to kill before this whole thing is over?"

"That was an accident, Trish. Nobody wanted him to die. Believe me, it wasn't intentional."

"Sure. I really believe that. Like I believe pigs fly."

"Well, maybe I can convince you. Meet me in half an hour at the Jefferson Memorial."

"Are you out of your fucking mind? You want me to meet a fucking killer at midnight without a soul around? Do you think

I'm out of my mind? No way am I falling for that load of bullshit!"

"That's too bad, Trish. We picked you because we thought you were a good reporter, someone who'd see the value of what's going on once it was fully explained."

"What do you mean?" she asked with less hostility.

"Like it or not, you're now a part of history. There's a lot more to this operation than the kidnapping and the pending attack on Iraq. I've got documentation that'll blow your mind."

"Why give it to me?" she asked, cautiously. "What purpose will giving it to me serve?

"When you see it, you'll understand," he reassured her. "I can't say anymore about it over the phone. If you want the info be at the memorial in thirty minutes. And," he quickly added, "don't tell anyone and be alone." The phone went dead.

Twenty-five minutes later Trish stepped from her car and walked nervously across the deserted parking lot towards the rear of the towering monument, gripping her mace can deep in her pocket. The biting wind made her glad she wore her heavy topcoat and knit cap. Upon reaching the path circling the monument, she paused and listened, expecting him to signal from among the swaying shadows. But she was met only by silence. Regretting her decision to come, she moved hesitantly toward the front of the monument and the sweeping steps leading up to the interior then abruptly changed her mind, and as a precaution went around the rear and approached from the far side, which was the less obvious route. As she rounded the corner the wind whipped her face and she jerked her collar up. Taking a deep breath, she moved deliberately along the narrow sidewalk, scanning the dark hedges to her right and the grove of barren cherry trees stretching into the night to her left, beyond the monument's perimeter of light. Spurts of adrenalin heightened her senses allowing her to isolate and discard the repetitious sound patterns from swaying branches and distant city noises carried across the frothy Tidal Basin.

At the steps, she paused and looked around. She was sure he was watching and waiting for her to make the climb before initiating contact. She checked the time and noted sourly that thirty minutes earlier she'd been secure and comfortable in her warm apartment and she wondered if she hadn't erred in deciding to pursue a career in journalism. She glanced up at the brightly lighted dome that stood in stark contrast against the moonless sky and began climbing, quickly at first then more cautiously. Half way up she stopped and turned hoping to see the man she was to meet coming up behind her. But there was no one. She glanced across the Tidal Basin at the luminous Washington Monument piercing the frigid night. It towered above her, she mused, as a silent witness to this foolish escapade. She took a deep breath and continued upward, sprinting two steps at a time. When she reached the final landing she felt invigorated and slightly more confident from the brief exertion. Again, she surveyed the area below and behind her before continuing inside. Standing high above the ground, exposed and unprotected, she shivered and drew her coat around her then turned and approached Jefferson's massive, bronze likeness. Craning up at the sculptured noble face made her feel small and vulnerable.

"Hello? Are you there?" she shouted. Instantly, her words were taken and dissipated by the wind. It was like shouting into a vacuum. A moment later, her query was answered by the straining engine of a passing semi down-shifting as it entered the Virginia-bound ramp of the 14th Street Bridge.

She had visited the monument many times before with friends and out of town guests but had never viewed it as she did this night. Looking around, she noted that the wide, floor-to-ceiling columns circling her provided excellent cover and that he could easily be concealed behind any one of them. Again, she called out, louder this time and with more urgency. "If you're there, let's get on with it. I'm freezing." Her anger rose with her impatience. Feeling bolder, she left the protection of Jefferson's shadow and walked deliberately around the expansive interior, peering around each column and daring him to come forward.

"Listen, damn it! It's late and I'm cold," she complained, irritably. "Let's get this over with," she shouted against her feeble echo.

She kept her gloved hands rammed deep inside her pockets as she moved angrily about, the left one clutching the mace, the other a Swiss Army knife, which she realized somewhat foolishly, would be useless against a professional killer. Moments later she was back at the base of the statue, huddled against the polished granite. For the first time, she regretted not calling Tom Sampson, a notion she'd considered fleetingly while dressing but then dismissed, fearing her phone was tapped. She checked her watch. Fifteen minutes had passed. She decided to give him fifteen minutes more.

The second quarter hour passed with excruciating slowness. To keep warm, she walked rapidly around Jefferson's feet, first clockwise, then reversed her pace. Several times she stopped abruptly, thinking she heard footsteps, only to be disappointed when she realized the sound was merely the echo of her own leather boots. Finally, thirty-five minutes after arriving, more angry than relieved, she ran down the steps, no longer caring whether or not anyone was lurking in the darkness and returned to her car.

Tired and irritable, Trish slammed the door to her apartment, threw her coat and hat on the sofa and kicked off her boots. She picked up the phone and checked for messages. There were none. Feeling foolish, she turned off the living room light and strode into her darkened bedroom, undressing as she walked. In her haste to depart she had left the bathroom light on and she now finished undressing by it, leaving her clothes where they fell. Naked, except for her panties, she crossed the room to her closet to retrieve her nightshirt. She opened the door, flipped the light switch and screamed.

Chapter Eleven

She called Sampson immediately. Though her words were incoherent, the message was clear and he was there within fifteen minutes. When he arrived she greeted him with red eyes. Still dazed and unable to speak, she simply raised her shaking hand and pointed toward the bedroom, which she refused to re-enter. Instead, she took refuge at the sofa, where she cradled her face in her hands and stared numbly ahead. He walked through the narrow hallway, stepping cautiously into the darkened bedroom, his Beretta drawn more from habit than necessity. His gaze went first to the bathroom. The water was still running and splotches of vomit clung to the basin. He switched on the overhead light with the nose of his gun and walked around her bed to the closet, stepping over her clothes as he moved.

Inside the closet Midshipman Zablocki stared at him from between her clothes, his head cocked $45°$ to the right, arms dangling at his sides. He was held in place by her pantyhose, which the killer had knotted tightly around his neck and fastened to the pole spanning the closet. Wedged between the knife handle and his chest was a page torn from *Jane's All the World's Aircraft*, the comprehensive reference book detailing every nation's military aircraft inventory and air war-fighting capabilities. This page portrayed technical data and photos of the U. S. F-16, the same aircraft Pickens had ordered into Turkey. Like Valerius, the mid's name tag had been removed. Without touching it Sampson recognized the K-Bar immediately. It was a standard Navy diving knife. The eight inch, stainless steel blade was set deep into the midshipman's chest. The lack of blood suggested he'd been murdered elsewhere and by other means. The FBI forensic team would be able to provide a clearer picture. But that was not as important as the two messages that had been sent. The one suggesting the F-16s be removed would have to be handled by the president. The other, was clearly intended for Sampson.

Special Agent Cutler and his team were as quick to respond to Sampson's call as he had been to Trish's. They entered the large apartment complex unobtrusively, toting their portable lab equipment in unmarked suitcases.

As the technicians worked around them, Sampson and Cutler huddled with Trish on the sofa, tenderly coaxing her out of her trauma to extract as much information as she could offer. Fortunately, her training as a reporter worked to their advantage and she painfully recounted the sequence of events beginning with the phone call earlier that evening. When she'd finished, Sampson helped her pack a few things and turned the apartment over to Cutler and his team. From there, he took her to his apartment.

While the other tenants slept, unaware of the gruesome crime scene, the agents gathered what little evidence there was and examined and photographed every aspect of Trish's place, transmitting much of the raw data back to FBI headquarters via a secure modem. They finished by 4:45 and, taking the body with them, were gone by 5:00.

At Sampson's urging the medical examiner had provided Trish with sedatives. Now, with her asleep in his bed, he spent the remainder of the pre-dawn morning on the phone calling in his men and notifying everyone up the chain of this newest development. His last call was to an office deep within the bowels of the J. Edgar Hoover building. The person with whom he spoke assured him the data he sought would be sent via secure phone to the Annapolis command center as quickly as possible.

The sun was breaking over the horizon when he finally concluded. It had been a long, disturbing night and he jumped into the shower to clear the cobwebs and to wash away some of the grime he felt from this latest slaying. Ten minutes later, dressed and armed, he checked on Trish. The sedatives had knocked her out and she lay there sleeping soundly with a tranquil expression that indicated the horror she'd experienced wasn't interfering with the rest she needed. The killer, he thought while studying her soft features, had needlessly put her through an excruciating ordeal. It would be one more debt he'd enjoy settling when the time came. With shards of morning light playing across the foot of the bed, he reached down and stroked her hair while gently raising the blanket to her shoulders. He thought they might have dinner somewhere in the Virginia countryside when this nightmare was over. At that moment she smiled as if aware of his thoughts and then rolled onto her side. There was a light but persistent knock at the door and he backed away, closing the bedroom door behind him.

"Morning, Fester," he said to his colleague, with a grateful nod at the large Dunkin' Donuts bag in his arms.

"Long night, eh?" came the low response.

Sampson nodded. "I can sure use that coffee."

In the cluttered dining room, he tore open the bag and grabbed one of the donuts. The caffeine and sugar fix kicked in and soon he was back to battery. As they ate, Sampson briefed his teammate on all that had happened and then concluded by disclosing the killer's identity. The revelation didn't surprise Fester, who, like Sampson, had served with him in Vietnam. But it did unsettle him.

"Stay with her as long as she needs you," Sampson said on his way out. "I don't trust that fucker. He may still come after her."

Fester was an avid rock climber and one of the more agile men on the team. With his martial arts and marksman training, he could easily take down three or four assailants at once. Yet, he respected and feared the man Sampson had tagged as the kidnapper and killer. So, the moment Sampson left, he double-locked the door and then, after checking in on Trish, chambered a round in his Glock and placed it on the coffee table between him and the front door. Picking up the morning paper, he settled in but his thoughts weren't on the headlines. They were back in the jungles of Vietnam.

Sampson, meanwhile, headed for Annapolis and a meeting with Harding.

He found the admiral drawn and pale but filled with anger.

"I want that bastard's balls, Tom," he shouted across the room as Sampson entered his office. He had just completed reading Cutler's initial report and he was seething.

The agent had stayed with the forensic crew, taking notes as they sorted and categorized their findings before faxing the raw data to Lucerne, Hemmings and Harding with the caveat that it was preliminary until verified. To Harding's way of thinking, no amount of verification was going to alter Zablocki's brutal death. His neck, according to the bureau, had been broken by a powerful twisting motion.

Seeing the report, Sampson asked, "What've you got there?" Unlike Harding, his temper was even and his voice as cold as stone. It was the way he operated in a combat environment. From day one, he had transitioned into a combat mode - functioning on automatic, without emotional distractions. It was a field-tested technique that enabled him to eliminate diversions which might otherwise cloud his judgment.

"Cutler's sitrep," the admiral replied. "It arrived a short while ago." Harding picked up the folder and handed it across the desk to the SEAL.

Scanning it, Sampson said, "Dead about twelve hours, eh? That tracks. Zablocki's corpse was taken to Mathews' place while she was spinning her wheels at the Jefferson Memorial. Sick motherfucker!"

"He can't get away with this," Harding fumed. "You've got to get him, Tom, before he kills again." The directive was more a plea than an order.

Sampson put the folder down. "Pardon me, admiral but you look like shit. You gonna be okay?"

"Don't worry about me," Harding snapped back. "You just concentrate on rescuing our mids." Then, retreating, he asked, "You want coffee?"

Sampson nodded and crossed the room to the thermos.

"I forgot," Harding said. "It's empty." Using the intercom, he asked for a refill. Moments later, an attendant appeared with another pot.

While he waited for the yeoman to pour out two cups and set the thermos on the credenza, Sampson studied the admiral and considered what he was about to tell him.

"I know who the killer is, admiral," he said, when the petty officer had left and closed the door behind him.

Harding nearly dropped his cup. Coffee spilled onto his desk and he asked, "Are you certain?"

"Yes, sir. It all came together when I found Zablocki. It was the way he was trussed up."

Harding folded his arms across his chest and leaned back. His slitted eyes were riveted on the man before him. This was more than he had expected.

"I've already said I believe he's one of us. Well, there's only one SEAL that would leave Zablocki's body that way. It pisses me off that I didn't think of him before. I guess, because as bad as he is, I never thought he'd stoop to this. His name's John Dankworth. We call him Bull."

"Jesus Christ!" Harding exclaimed. "I know him. I recommended him to court martial several years ago when I was on the CNO's staff."

"I know," Sampson replied with a nod.

"He got three years at Leavenworth for smuggling drugs into New Mexico during the Contra uprisings," Harding recalled. "But why do you think it's him?"

"He liked playing games with the VC during the war. One of his tricks was to string a few up by the neck on a long pole and torture them in front of their comrades to get them to talk. He justified it as psychological warfare. And I suppose it was. But he also enjoyed it. He had a unique way of tying them up..., always with the same knot. Said he picked it up from a Filipino warrior in jungle training. It was the one used on Zablocki."

Harding sat frozen as Sampson went on describing Dankworth's wartime activities.

"He was sick. After trussing them up, he'd cut off a body part - a foot, hand, cock, arm - it didn't matter. Whatever amused him or had the greatest shock value. Then he'd force the others to eat it. Once, he even cut out a guy's heart. Toward the end of the

97

war, during covert ops across the border in Laos and Cambodia, he started cutting off their balls and hanging them from his belt."

Harding made no attempt to hide his disgust.

"There was one SEAL in his company," Sampson went on, "a junior officer, very religious, who vowed to turn him in once they got back to Nam if he didn't knock it off." Sampson gulped the rest of his coffee before continuing. "One night our guys, along with a squad of Cambodian guerrillas were patrolling a river bank. Their scouts reported a line of VC sampans with supplies coming towards them. They repositioned downriver with Dankworth and some men moving to the opposite shore. Then they hunkered down and waited. The fire fight lasted about five minutes. All the VC were killed and so was the officer. He took a large round in the head that scattered his brains over half the delta."

Harding asked reluctantly, "Dankworth?"

"There's been scuttlebutt over the years. Rumors he recrossed the river before the shooting started. But no proof."

"What do you think?"

"I think he did it," Sampson replied.

"Where is he now, Tom? Where's that sonofabitch now?" Harding said through clenched teeth.

"I don't know. But, I'm working on it. In fact," he glanced at his watch, "I may have some info for you shortly. Now, if you'll excuse me, admiral, I've got a meeting with my troops in fifteen minutes."

As he stood to leave Harding stopped him. "Wait. I know what you're thinking. Dankworth's getting even with me. Isn't he?"

Sampson nodded. "It occurred to me."

Harding looked shaken. "Those mids didn't have to die."

"You can't blame yourself, admiral. This guy's a maverick. A nut case."

The words didn't seem to help. He was awash with guilt.

"We'll get him, admiral," Sampson promised.

Harding nodded but it was clear he was now carrying an added burden. Then, as he came from around his desk, he said,

"Get back to me as soon as you've got anything. Anything. You hear?"

"Aye, aye, sir."

Returning to his car, Sampson wondered what Harding's reaction would be if he knew that in addition to seeking revenge against him, that Dankworth was also luring Sampson into a trap. He knew the ex-SEAL better than most men in their small community. They'd trained and fought together for more than twenty years. It was Dankworth, the senior of the two, who, upon being tasked to create a counter-terrorist force that would be superior to any already in existence, had recruited Sampson as his executive officer. It was a natural selection, since both men shared the same war fighting skills and enjoyed a close friendship, that is, until Sampson later refused to go along with the cocaine deal.

He knew Bull had interpreted his refusal as an inexcusable breach of their unique bond, one that fused all SEALs together, and which subsequently led to his court martial and jail time. In Bull's tangled mind, Sampson should have backed him up after he'd committed to the Mafia to deliver pure cocaine to them while the SEALs were training Contras in their war against the Sandanistas. In trying to persuade him to go along, Dankworth had asserted that it was a beautiful setup. With unrestricted access to isolated airstrips in Arizona and New Mexico, transporting the drugs on trips north while picking up arms for the Contras was a once-in-a-lifetime opportunity. For warriors like them, who had put their lives on the line countless times, this was a unique chance to acquire money that was long due them. It was all clean money, he had argued. Money that would never see the inside of a U.S. bank.

At first, Dankworth had tried reasoning with his colleague and when that failed he played on their friendship. Throughout their heated discussions, neither man mentioned his mounting debts or his two families; the wife and daughter in San Diego and a second wife and a son in the Philippines. Until then, maintaining both households had been easy. His Navy salary went to his American family and the money from the bar he and his Filipina wife owned in Olongapo, just outside the Subic Bay naval base, more than covered their expenses. But all that changed when the Navy was forced out of the Philippines and the income from the bar dried up. At the time, smuggling seemed to be the best, if not the only solution to his problems.

When Sampson rejected his repeated overtures, Dankworth turned to the man who ultimately caved in under DEA pressure and set him up. The result was catastrophic for Bull. He lost everything - his Navy career, both wives and most of all, his one chance at grabbing the big one. Sampson would never forget Dankworth's penetrating stare when he'd been called to testify. He knew then he'd made an enemy for life.

Dankworth had disappeared after completing his sentence. That was two years ago. There were rumors among the SEALs that he'd relocated to New York, where he was offering his services to North African nations through their emissaries at the United Nations. It was based on that hearsay that Sampson had called the FBI's Criminal Records Division earlier that morning.

Now, driving across the Severn River to the command center, he thought of how his former teammate was deliberately drawing him into a trap. Both men had considerable legal and criminal training that included interpreting and manipulating forensic evidence. They had often used those skills to alter the scene of battles against terrorist strongholds so they wouldn't be accused of using excess force. To avoid criminal charges and law suits they had to ensure it appeared they killed only in self defense. The ironclad rule when storming terrorist fortresses was to leave no terrorists alive who could later testify against them in court. But even without eyewitnesses the evidence could convict them. To alter it, they had to act fast. Before signalling the all clear to local authorities, they would reposition bodies and vary firing positions to lead investigators to conclude every death was justified. Sometimes weapons would have to be placed in dead hands and fired. It had been Dankworth's idea to acquire those skills as a way of protecting themselves from spineless politicians who might later capitulate to screaming liberals and make scapegoats out of them. With that sensitivity to details, Sampson knew Dankworth would never leave a trail of clues unintentionally. There was only one conclusion - he wanted Sampson to know it was he who had kidnapped and killed the mids.

He pulled up to the low, gray building and noted from the cars in the lot that his team had arrived. He entered and showed his ID to the guard.

"Anything for me?" he asked the officer on duty in the command center.

"Yes, Commander," the Chief Petty Officer replied. "This came in from FBI Headquarters about thirty minutes ago." He handed him a sealed envelope marked *Urgent*.

Sampson took it and headed for his office, picking up a cup of coffee on the way. While his men crowded into the small office he read the message, then placed it squarely on the desk before him.

He studied his team for a long moment then, without wasting words, he said, "We got a real can of worms here, fellas." He was more pensive than usual. "Our kidnapper's one of us." There was a stirring but no one responded. "Everything points to Bull Dankworth."

Someone murmured,"Jesus Christ!" while the others accepted the news with ponderous silence. Most knew Dankworth personally, a few only by reputation. He'd personally recruited many of them when putting the team together. With carte blanche from the top brass he'd been able to choose any man he wanted from among the other established SEAL teams, angering his contemporaries in the process, which doubly pleased him. Dankworth enjoyed rubbing noses in the dirt, particularly of those men who didn't measure up to his own curious standards. By his reasoning, he was entitled to the best the Navy had to offer and if he could create some dissent while doing so, all the better.

Not everyone came from the other teams. Some, bored when the fighting in Vietnam ended, had left the Navy in search of other wars. Those, he'd tracked down and lured back, promising action and thrills only warriors understood and appreciated.

"It gets worse, guys," Sampson added. "He's raised the stakes. Not only is he working for the Iranians, he's turned this into a personal vendetta. He wants my head and he'll take down anyone in the way - which means, you." He then explained how the ex-SEAL was leading them to him.

Reading from the FBI report he'd just received, he went on to brief them on the man they'd soon meet in combat.

"According to the bureau's files, our boy began courting Algerian and Egyptian fundamentalists after graduating Leavenworth. He was careful to conduct his affairs within the law, making no attempt to hide or disguise his business dealings with them. He began by establishing personal security services for foreign officials and wealthy businessmen coming to America. All very legal. Then, later, he expanded abroad with an office in Nicosia, Cyprus, where he went out of his way to stay clean. According to this," he said, referring to the report, "he even established contact with the resident CIA agent there and volunteered to keep him informed of his dealings and movements."

"Yeah. Knowing full well, with his clients they would've kept him under surveillance anyway," Cort said derisively. "He gives `em just enough info to keep them off his back."

"That's how he operates," Sampson agreed. "Bull establishes a pattern that lulls everyone into a false sense of security. Meanwhile, the fucker's using his clients as a cover."

"He doesn't want to become another Edwin Wilson," Cort said, referring to the turncoat American intelligence officer whose carelessness in establishing terrorist training camps in Libya landed him in an American jail for life, but not before he provided Ghadaffi with enough plastic explosives to arm every dissident on the African continent.

"Do you think," one of the younger SEALs asked, "he's been using Cyprus as a jumping off point to enter other countries?"

"I'm sure that's exactly what he's been doing," Sampson said. "Cyprus' loose borders and convenient location makes it ideal for skipping around the Med undetected."

"And," Cort reminded them, "crossing borders is one of Bull's specialties. For those who don't know him, he's a master at disappearing without leaving tracks. With the help of the local bad guys, becoming invisible is a piece of cake for him."

"It gets better," Sampson continued. "Dankworth dropped out of sight two months before the World Trade Center bombing. He packed up and closed his offices and hasn't been seen or heard of since. According to FBI transcripts of the tapes made by their informant when the radicals were plotting the bombing, there are obscure references to someone who is likely our boy." Reading from the report, he said, "This says the sheik and his comrades repeatedly spoke of their main man, who they called Mr. B, and who was available to them through Nicosia and Tunis. Despite the indictments and subsequent convictions, the FBI is convinced they haven't captured the chief architect of a terror campaign which they now know was supposed to go beyond the Trade Center to include assassinating Egypt's president, bombing the UN, the FBI's New York headquarters, two tunnels and a bridge connecting New Jersey with Manhattan and - you ready for this? - kidnappings in the nation's capital."

As the team pondered the news one man asked, "Where's this taking us? If Dankworth's our man, then what's next?"

"We continue narrowing our search for the bastard," Sampson replied. "But," he added, thoughtfully, "I don't think we're going to find him until he's ready."

Chapter Twelve

"You sonofabitch! You're fucking with my son's life!" were the first words out of Bennett's mouth when he heard Pickens come on the line. "What the hell do you think you're doing moving aircraft around that god forsaken region? Do you have any idea of what you hope to accomplish, Les? I thought we had an understanding that you were going to let those bastards fight it out among themselves and then take the credit for Saddam's downfall. What happened?"

"Please, Russ, take it easy. Don't get overwrought." Pickens sounded weak and unconvincing. "We've got to have contingencies," he explained. "We can't just allow them to move in without having some options. You should know that best of all."

"Don't patronize me, you bastard. I'll tell you what I know best of all." He lowered his voice but there was no mistaking his anger. "My son's life is hanging in the balance while you play idiotic war games with a bunch of fanatics who don't give a rat's ass about anything but settling old scores. I just learned about his other classmate and I can't help worrying that he'll be next. In case you haven't figured it out, Les, they're not going to put up with much more of your foolishness. Life isn't precious to them. They're ready to die for Allah and if we're not careful they'll take my son with them."

"I don't think we have to worry about that, Russ. Your son's worth more to them alive."

His feeble attempt to assuage Bennett only angered him.

"That's exactly your goddamn problem, Les. You don't think! Who's been counseling you this time, that numbskull wife of yours?"

"Now, Russ, there's, er, no need for that kind of talk. We're all friends here."

Melissa Pickens' raw political appetite was no secret. Nor was her usurpation of some of the president's prerogatives as she struggled to gain a toe-hold on the national scene that would enable her to further her own political agenda. Most of official Washington willingly allowed her some leeway because of her husband's shortcomings as long as her aggressiveness didn't interfere with their own plans or threatened their power bases. Of late, however, she had pushed too hard on the Hill and was finding mounting resistance even among her own party's more liberal members, which included Bennett when it came to domestic issues.

"You're a damn fool," Bennett reprimanded. "After nearly three years in office you still haven't learned on which side your bread is buttered. I didn't think it necessary to remind you that I've carried you through a lot of skirmishes and taken a lot of heat along the way. I thought you were smart enough to at least remember your allies, Les. Smart enough to grasp the significance of my counsel on this issue and then follow it."

Pickens winced at each barb. His head pounded and his stomach ached.

"Smart enough to know not to cross this line. Obviously," he hissed, "I was mistaken. You're a stupid ass." He spoke slowly, allowing Pickens to absorb the full impact of what was about to follow, not caring that McCurdy was dutifully monitoring their conversation. "Now, see if you can fathom what I'm telling you, son. If my boy doesn't survive this ordeal because of your foolishness I'll bring you and that pompous wife of yours down so hard future historians will use your name as a synonym for `shit.' I hope I've made myself clear."

"Yes. Yes you have, Russ. Perfectly."

Pickens continued holding the receiver after Bennett abruptly severed their connection. After a long while, he lowered the phone and shifted his thoughts to his meeting with Lucerne and the others, just hours away. With Bennett's threats still echoing in his ears, it was not something he was looking forward to.

Gartland and Lucerne arrived minutes before Hemmings. All three gathered in the reception room beyond the Oval Office. They were armed with the intelligence update which they hoped would convince Pickens to augment the forces he'd pre-positioned in the region earlier. But when they saw Pickens' high state of anxiety they each concluded that things didn't look promising. Usually the president would came from behind his desk to greet them but this time he remained there, keeping it between them like a shield.

Nodding, he waved them toward the chairs set before him and said, without meeting their gaze, "Good afternoon, gentlemen. Please be seated."

McCurdy, who was more somber than usual, waited for the others then took the chair to the president's right.

"It was a terrible thing that happened to that other young cadet," Pickens offered, his thoughts seemingly elsewhere. Turning, he asked McCurdy, "What's his name?"

Seething, Lucerne answered before the chief of staff, using the opportunity to correct Pickens' use of the term cadet. "*Midshipman* Firstclass Zablocki, sir," he said, forcefully. "Louis K. Zablocki."

Pickens caught the inference and shifted. "Yes that's it. Simply horrible. Has the family been notified?"

Again, it was Lucerne who responded. "Not yet. Like Valerius' family we're holding off until this situation is resolved. Both bodies are being held in the morgue at Quantico. As long as you brought it up, Mr. President, I recommend that after initial notification has been made you consider a private ceremony here in the White House for the families. It would be the right thing to do," he added bitterly.

"Certainly, general. It shall be done. Now," he said, with a nod to the Secretary of Defense, "please tell me what you've learned about this mess we're in."

"We've just received a shocking revelation," he said. "The leader of the Navy's Red Cell is convinced the man responsible for the kidnappings and three murders is himself an ex-SEAL."

"That's incredible!" Pickens exclaimed with genuine surprise. "What makes him think so?"

"There's enough evidence to suggest it, Mr. President. Specifically, the way the two recent murders have been carried out," Gartland didn't feel a need to provide the details. "It also appears he may have been one of the principals in the World

107

Trade Center bombing. And, what's more incredible is that he's a convicted felon who, in all likelihood, sold his services to the Iranians and, in addition to doing their dirty work, is now carrying out his own personal vendetta against specific members of the naval service, including the very man charged with hunting him down."

Pickens shook his head. "It reads like a gruesome novel. I wonder where it's all going to end."

"Well, if we prevail," Hemmings offered, "it should end with this man's capture and the rescue of our mids. I know Commander Sampson, the man heading our rescue team, and if anyone can bring this monster in, Sampson's the man to do it."

"That's reassuring," Pickens said, rubbing his temples. "I hope he succeeds quickly. Anymore on the mids' status before moving on to the gulf situation?"

"That's it for now," Gartland replied, shooting a quick glance at McCurdy.

All three shared the aide's concern for Pickens' erratic behavior and his growing inability to focus on specifics beyond core issues. Accordingly, at McCurdy's suggestion they had agreed not to clutter the agenda with extraneous details, believing it was critical that Pickens not withdraw any further from the problem or, worse still, yield to Bennett.

Hemmings began with a summary of the most recent intelligence gathered from satellites and other sources. His tone, while even, held a hint of urgency. "We're observing what I'd characterize as a secondary massing of forces in Iran's northeastern sector, most of it about two days drive from Iraq's border. Not surprising, the activity exceeds anything we're accustomed to seeing at this time of year. Of more concern though, are the movements in the south."

As he spoke, Pickens fidgeted with his pencil.

"All ships now in port are lighting off their radars and communications antennas. This," Hemmings explained, "is what we would expect of them prior to getting underway."

"They've obviously learned a lesson or two about not keeping ships in port during a war," Lucerne inserted. Then, in response to the president's confused look, he added, "You may recall that our naval forces knocked out a few of their ships during the 1988 Tanker War."

The president didn't respond and Hemmings continued, "Furthermore, there's a dramatic increase of heavy truck traffic at their two major gulf bases, Bander Abbas and Boushehr, where ships can be seen taking on large quantities of munitions and supplies. Additionally, tanks have already been loaded aboard amphibious ships and troops are embarking as we speak. Yesterday, several smaller naval craft were repositioned to smaller bases at Khorramshar and Kharg Island, joining eleven fast attack missile boats and fourteen hovercraft already positioned there." He paused briefly, allowing Pickens to visualize what he had just said.

"Sounds like they mean business," Pickens said as he withdrew his handkerchief and wiped the corners of his mouth.

"It would seem so. There's more, Mr. President," Hemmings said. "They're dispersing their aircraft as a precaution, including their Su-24 Fencers, which are of particular concern to us, Mr. President." Hemmings then clarified, "...because of their air-to-surface capability. We're also picking up a noticeable increase in communications between Tehran and their military echelons. The intel we're getting from HUMINT sources reveals they're planning to attack from the north, which is the traditional invasion route, with a small, highly concentrated diversionary force, while using their main forces to strike Iraq's soft underbelly, which as you know was weakened by the 1991 Gulf War."

Finally, Hemmings paused and Pickens asked him, "Is that as much as we know?"

"Pretty much," he replied, flatly, not wanting to burden the president with technical details that would add nothing to the scenario. "With the strait closed and our surface forces re-located to the southern sector of the Arabian Sea as you ordered, Iran can strike when ready."

"You haven't mentioned their latest demands," Pickens said, referring to the typed note recovered from Zablocki's shirt pocket, directing a withdrawal of the F-16s. "We can't ignore them without endangering another midshipman." But he didn't wait for a response. Instead, he turned to Gartland and said, "I appreciate what you're telling me but I think its best to return the F-16s and support aircraft we've moved into the area back to their Mediterranean bases immediately. I also want the Saratoga repositioned to the Ionian Sea, off southern Italy. Further, I want our contingent of army and air force advisors out of Saudi Arabia, as we've been directed to do."

He paused and wiped the edges of his mouth again. Then, clearing his throat, he said, "I've given this considerable thought, gentlemen, and I believe the best course of action is to show Iran we mean to let them settle their regional differences without outside interference. Over a million Iranians died in the 1979 war with Iraq, many horribly from chemical weapons. Iran has every right to move against its historical enemy, particularly when that enemy has been weakened, ironically by a war of its own choosing. We don't have the wherewithal or the moral authority to prevent neighbors from settling their differences. Admittedly, what makes this decision attractive is that by standing aside, Saddam, who continues to be a thorn in our side and a threat to the region, may well be eliminated. We dropped the ball once when we had the chance and I don't wish to repeat that mistake this time. I sincerely appreciate your inclination that Iran poses a greater threat to world order than Iraq and your advice to act accordingly. But, I don't agree.

"General Lucerne, you have demonstrated in our deliberations that you, more than anyone involved in this decision, are willing to sacrifice what you hold near and dear for the sake of what you perceive is best for America. I certainly find no fault with your motives. In fact, I laud them. However, in this instance, I must overrule you in the hope that in doing so we are able to retrieve our midshipmen without interfering with the natural order of international relations. I grant you that it's a gamble. But, I believe it to be the best course of action for America and the world community."

Touching his stomach, he shifted in his seat and said, "If you have nothing further for me, I consider this meeting concluded."

This latest reversal had Bennett written all over it. And it disturbed the three advisors that Pickens had allowed him to cloud his vision and not grasp the implications of a gulf war that would result in a strengthening of Iran's Revolutionary Guard.

As they left a troubled president behind, they took some comfort in knowing they had at least one concealed asset still available to them.

Chapter Thirteen

Alerted by JCS intelligence sitreps to the increasing activity at Iran's naval bases, Commander Dan Cherico extended his sub's operating area northward, off the coast of Bushehr to better monitor shipping traffic out of the base closest to Iraq. The first day's patrol revealed only a high level of activity among small harbor and coastal craft. Then, late the second day the Annapolis' sensors detected several underwater craft departing the harbor at fifteen minute intervals.

"How many have we counted so far?" Cherico asked his ops officer.

"Five, skipper. The last one exited twenty-five minutes ago on the same course and speed as the others. That may have been the last. We're not picking up any signs of further egress in the harbor, sir. Looks like the others aren't going on this excursion."

The deployment of Iran's midget subs disturbed Cherico. As he studied their positions on the chart before him, he mechanically stroked his blonde handlebar moustache, the only departure from Navy grooming standards he tolerated on his boat during deployments.

Though this was Dan Cherico's first command at sea he understood that crew morale was a critical element for safety and efficiency. So, when the Chief of the Boat suggested relaxing the rules on their extended deployment to permit moustaches, he agreed. Commissioned a year after the Persian Gulf War, in April 1992, the Annapolis was one of Navy's newer Los Angeles class nuclear submarines. And, while many of its crew had served aboard the other eleven subs that had participated in that war, including the two that had fired Tomahawk land attack missiles into Iraq from the eastern Mediterranean, Cherico insisted on his own brand of training that reflected a deep respect for the dangers of life aboard a submarine. From his first day aboard, he drilled them with missionary zeal, beginning with their pre-deployment phase and then, harder still at sea. Throughout their arduous workup, he remained steadfast to his rule of never expecting more from them than he was prepared to give. As a result, re-enlistments had reached new heights and the 133-man crew ranked among the top in fleet-wide advancement exams. Likewise, they had scored high in the fleet commander's gruelling operational readiness evaluations.

For Cherico, his crew was his family and at sea he maximized his time with them, quizzing them daily about the boat and its mission. His goal was to prepare each man of the *A-Team*, as he called them, for future leadership responsibilities. By the time the Annapolis entered the Persian Gulf his entire ops crew knew the naval order of battle of each country within their operating area. They knew, too, that the Iranian midget subs were of North Korean design and first delivered to Iran in June 1988 as part of a twenty-four package deal. They also knew Iran had taken possession of nineteen to date, that each was capable of diving 328 feet and could deliver bottom laid mines, or the more deadly limpets, which could be attached to hulls and piers by divers exiting from specially designed side compartments. But what no one aboard the Annapolis knew as they tracked them, including their skipper, was their destination and mission.

"What's their course?" Cherico queried his ops officer.

"Unless they intend altering course later on, they don't appear to be heading where I had expected," the officer replied. "They're holding to 260 , which will put them south of Iraq," he said, pointing to the chart. "Looks like they're heading for Safaniya, Saudi Arabia. What do you make of it, skipper?"

"Could be they want to stay in friendly waters as long as possible before proceeding on. Or...," he mused as he tugged on his moustache. "Then again, it could be Iraq isn't their target. We'll have to be patient."

Six hours later, Cherico received a call over the intercom.

"Ops to Conn."

"Conn, aye," he replied.

"Skipper, they're dispersing," the ops officer alerted with obvious concern. "Bravo One is heading north toward Kuwait, Bravo Two is maintaining the original heading and Bravos Three, Four and Five are fanning off to the south."

"Roger," Cherico replied before turning to the conning officer and directing him to change course. "Stay with Bravo One," he ordered. "And maintain four thousand yards distance."

For the next several hours the Annapolis monitored the midgets as they seeded mines along the Kuwaiti and Saudi coastlines. Hiding within the irregular coastal thermal layers, the seven thousand ton submarine glided steadily south, careful not to disclose its presence while noting along the way the precise locations the midgets lingered as they seeded the entrances to naval and coast guard ports with mines. Anticipating the subs would retrace their course after completing their mission, Cherico remained with Bravo Five off Saudi Arabia's southern coast and followed it back to where it rendezvoused with the others before returning to Bushehr.

From there, the Annapolis shadowed them to within a mile of Bushehr, monitoring their movements until the last midget re-entered port. As the sub prepared to withdraw to deeper waters ops reported two fast approaching ships.

"We got visitors, skipper," the ops officer announced, calmly. "Sounds like frigates and, if I didn't know better, I'd say they were after us."

Cherico checked the time. It was twenty hours since he'd filed his last situation report and nearing time for the next one. Unlike his previous message, which confirmed much of what he knew the Pentagon could determine from satellite imagery, this one would reveal Iran was targeting more than the Iraqis.

"Okay. Let's go passive. All stop," he ordered. Turning to his navigator, he said, "Give me a precise location."

Above them the frigates reduced speed and began maneuvering in a manner that suggested to Cherico they might be conducting ASW ops. For ninety tense minutes the ships remained directly overhead before suddenly heading south.

Undeterred, Cherico fell discretely behind them and followed to where they were joined by two of Iran's three destroyers, two corvettes and a replenishment ship. The formation then resumed a northerly course while maneuvering erratically along Iran's coastline in what he determined was underway refresher training.

At that point the Annapolis turned and fell back away from the formation. At precisely midnight, her periscope broke the surface. The message detailing the midgets' mission and identifying the coordinates of their separate op areas had been written and encoded hours earlier. In less than fifteen seconds the sophisticated five-inch periscope-mounted dish stabilized itself and locked onto the 10,000 pound, geosynchronous Milstar satellite, orbiting thousands of miles in space. Below the churning waves, far beyond enemy detection, the ship's communications officer confirmed uplink and pressed the button that transmitted a four-second squirt of digital communications containing 1,500,000 bits per second over an Ultra High Frequency with laser accuracy. Simultaneously, the Annapolis received a similar squirt over a Super High Frequency which had been sent hours earlier by Lucerne and stored in the satellite. Coded specifically for the Annapolis, it remained there until retrieved. The entire sequence lasted a minute. With her periscope once again retracted, the A-Team resumed their silent vigil.

Chapter Fourteen

The National Security Council convened on the heels of two urgent messages received just hours apart. The first, from the USS Annapolis, was retrieved by one of the Pentagon's numerous rooftop satellite dishes minutes after being transmitted from the depths of the Persian Gulf. The second, originated in Riyadh at the American Embassy. That one set off alarm bells in the State Department's Crisis Center.

In the White House basement the dimmed overhead lights accentuated the ocher glow that illuminated the somber faces of the men arrayed before the wall-sized back lit screen depicting a military-oriented map of the Persian Gulf. Lucerne began by delineating the disposition of Iran's armed forces with particular attention to its deployed naval forces and the recently sown mine fields, while the president suppressed his anger at learning of the sub's presence in the gulf.

"How can we be certain those midgets were actually laying mines?" he asked, truculently, searching to discredit Lucerne's analysis.

"Evaluated independently, one might make the case they were engaged in oceanographic surveys," Lucerne conceded with restrained sarcasm. "But," he added in an unyielding tone, "viewed in the larger context of everything else we know, Mr. President, we'd be extremely naive to accept that theory."

"Yes, but there's still the possibility they didn't actually lay mines. Would you concede they may have been on a reconnaissance mission or perhaps conducting training in preparation for invading Iraq?" Pickens was doing his utmost to keep from deserting Bennett.

"Possible, but not likely when one considers the report from Riyadh." Lucerne would have liked to add, "You dumb sonofabitch." But, of course, he didn't. Instead, he held his silence while Pickens displayed his resentment at having to defend what was obviously turning into a losing position.

"Then let's press on with it," the president said, coolly.

Lucerne glanced across the table to Harrison, the Deputy Secretary of State, as he shuffled papers before him.

Taking his clue, Harrison cleared his throat and immediately offered, "As General Lucerne has indicated, Mr. President, we have disturbing news from our ambassador further suggesting we may have been hoodwinked by the Iranians."

"Aw, Jesus," Pickens said without attempting to hide his disappointment. Then, under his breath, he said, "Where the hell's it going to stop?"

Continuing, Harrison went on to report, "In the past twenty-four hours, representatives of the Ayatollah have made serious allegations and threats to Saudi's religious leaders which, in the face of what has transpired in the gulf, cannot be dismissed or taken lightly."

Harrison was a slight, balding man who had reached the second highest position at State through a long and distinguished career in the Foreign Service. A Harvard man, he was one of the few carryovers from the previous administration, who Pickens had wisely retained temporarily for continuity while his less experienced political appointees struggled to define America's new foreign policy in the post-soviet world order. Unable to formulate a unified strategy to adequately address the power vacuum created by the disintegrating former Soviet Union and the emergence of the new European Union, along with the economic tidal wave tearing Asia and South America apart and an Africa embroiled in undulating political upheaval, Pickens finally dismissed all thoughts of putting the veteran diplomat out to pasture.

Harrison's pronounced New England accent and resonant voice filled the small briefing room.

"Citing documented evidence of increasing human rights abuses by the present regime, including suppression of freedom of expression and political association," he said, referring to the cable before him, "Iran's Mullahs have labeled the Royal Family enemies of Islam, accusing them of a hypocritical lifestyle that smacks of double standards. They go on to condemn the Saudi king for systematically subduing his subjects while extracting the Holy Land's wealth and resources for his personal gain. Furthermore, they claim, he has betrayed the Koran by repeatedly instigating riots at Islam's two holy sites in order to justify implementing heavy-handed police tactics and legitimizing unreasonably harsh border restrictions during pilgrimages, thus preventing the faithful from fulfilling their obligations to visit Mecca. Citing the king's gross malfeasance, mismanagement and abuse of his custodial responsibilities, Iran contends the king and his family have lost all rights to serve Islam."

Harrison sipped from his water glass, enabling the president, who seemed otherwise occupied, to absorb the full implications of Iran's accusations.

"Additionally, Mr. President, Iran asserts, by entering into a partnership with western powers, the Royal Family has become unwitting puppets of the Great Satan which, in Iran's judgment, maligns the teachings of Allah. Iran goes on to charge the king and his family with acting in opposition to regional hegemony by allowing the U. S. to stockpile military arms and equipment within their borders. Equipment, which they maintain has been used in the past to suppress Islamic nations and undoubtedly will be again in the future. They have denounced the Saudis for channelling fortunes derived from the people's natural resources into the pockets of western arms dealers in exchange for weapons they themselves intend to use to further subdue the Saudi people. And, finally, they have accused the Royal Family of conspiring with Israel to undermine Palestinian progress in their goal to establish a self-ruling homeland."

"Sounds like their singing from the same old song sheet," Pickens said, dismissively.

"It would be a mistake to classify it as the same idle rhetoric they've spewed in the past, Mr. President," Diamond, the National Security Advisor quickly countered. "In the context of Iran's current domestic situation, we must interpret these threats against

Saudi Arabia much more seriously," he said, nodding to the CIA Director seated across from him.

They were working in concert now, coming at him from all sides. It was Hemmings turn and he began, "In that regard, Mr. President, recent intelligence indicates political infighting in Iran has reached new heights. Opposition to the president's efforts to move toward a market economy by privatizing Iran's sprawling bureaucracy is now openly confrontational. For the first time since the Shah's reign, conservative religious leaders are publicly vilifying the president in what can only be described as an obstructionist parliament. Until recently, he's been a voice of reason in Iran but his power is rapidly waning.

"As you know," Hemmings added, fully aware Pickens' knowledge of the region was extremely limited, "under their constitution, the president, despite his ranking as a senior cleric, can't run for a third term. We believe his inability to reverse the country's spiraling economy and his lame duck tenure are the root causes for Iran's decision to pursue its oft-stated expansionist goals. For confirmation, we need only look at their recent annexation of the Abu Mesa, Sirra and Farsi Islands which, until recently, they controlled jointly with the United Arab Emirates." Hemmings stifled, "Thanks in part to our own dissipated military." Instead, he continued, "The charges against the Royal Family are a clear indication the Ayatollah has garnered enough political power to usurp the president's constitutional authority and is orchestrating an attack against Saudi Arabia under the religious pretense of wresting Mecca and Medina from their corrupt stewards."

"And, what of their stated intent to invade Iraq?" Pickens asked.

It was Lucerne's turn. "There isn't going to be any. It was a ruse. They've tricked us into withdrawing our forces to avoid a confrontation that would justify our intrusion."

"In a nutshell, Mr. President," Diamond said, "they feared we'd retaliate if any of our forces were attacked or threatened during the assault phase of the operation. Now, without that prospect, the likelihood of the American electorate supporting our involvement has been considerably diminished. Furthermore, lacking serious opposition they're now positioned to move swiftly against the Saudis. If they aren't deterred, Mr. President, it'll be over before we can react. You may recall, it took nearly six months of sustained logistical ops to position adequate forces and equipment in that region before we could strike at Iraq in 1991."

"Are you telling me we have no options against a hostile takeover of sixty percent of the world's known oil reserves?" He spread his hands out beseechingly on the table, his tense voice betraying the alarm bells ringing in his head. "Certainly, if the situation is as bad as you describe, we must have some line of defense. What about our submarine, general?" he asked with a renewed sense of urgency while pushing away the untouched platter of cookies.

Had the matter not been so serious, Lucerne would have relished twisting Pickens' tail before coming to his aid. Instead, he said, "Though our options are limited, Mr. President, we still have a few cards we can play."

Pickens' facial muscles tightened at Lucerne's gentle prod. "And what might they be?" he asked, gritting his teeth.

On cue, the Persian Gulf regional map was replaced by one encompassing a larger segment of the globe that included portions of the Indian Ocean to the south and the eastern Mediterranean to the north. Overlaying it were a series of red concentric circles emanating out from the center of Iran.

"Beginning with our farthest assets on the outer circle," Lucerne said turning his attention to the screen, "the Kitty Hawk Battle Group is lingering in the vicinity of Diego Garcia."

His words prompted an aide to superimpose a blinking arrow on that segment of the map.

"We can reposition them to the central Arabian Sea, beyond Iran's detection, in seventy-two hours," he said. As he spoke the arrow traced a northwesterly path along the 1,400-mile sea route toward the gulf.

Anticipating Pickens' questions, Lucerne next provided an overview of the task group's capabilities as ship and aircraft silhouettes corresponding to the task force appeared in the upper right hand section of the screen.

"The embarked air wing is more than adequately configured with attack and fighter aircraft to handle any tasking we may assign her. The battle group's Aegis cruisers and destroyers are armed with Tomahawk, Standard and ASROC missiles that will counter any air, surface, subsurface or land-based target. Say the word, and they'll start steaming north.

"Next, we can position AWACS and long range tankers at these locations to support land-based attack aircraft."

Again, a series of blinking arrows appeared across the screen at airfields in Diego Garcia, Turkey and Italy.

"And, finally," he said with an imperceptible grin, "there's the Annapolis, which is armed with Tomahawk, conventional land-attack missiles as well as anti-ship Harpoon missiles, torpedoes and a contingent of SEALs. She alone can inflict enough damage to give Iran second thoughts about invading Saudi Arabia." He paused briefly, then added, "As you can see, Mr. President, we're not impotent." He didn't say what he and the others were thinking, "Given those assets, do you have the balls to stand up to the Iranians?"

Again, Bennett's angry words filled Pickens' head as he stared at the pulsating map and weighed the military options before him. Had he been included in the meeting, Pickens knew his friend and mentor would be forcefully arguing his case to stay the course despite the overwhelming evidence that Iran's intentions were not what they had initially portrayed them to be. While searching the faces before him, Pickens knew he would have yielded to Bennett's will and stood aside if it were just the two nations evening old scores. Bennett had been persuasive in convincing him that on the grand scale, it mattered little what happened between the two Middle Eastern countries. A war, he had asserted, served only to further weaken their enemies' failing economies, thereby strengthening America's position in the region. Provided the battle was confined to Iran and Iraq and didn't spill over into the major oil producing countries or affect their ability to produce and trade, Bennett had argued, they could kill each other until the cows came home.

Now, Pickens reflected, by Bennett's own admission, the stakes had been raised by Iran. In light of these new developments his friend couldn't blame him for yielding to Lucerne and the others. After all, Bennett's argument had become moot in the face of Iran's bellicose threats to the Saudis and the mining of their ports, which, as Diamond had diligently pointed out, was in of itself, an act of war.

"How do we proceed?" Pickens asked with resignation.

As Lucerne was about to tell him, an aide, who had been called from the room earlier returned and handed the general a slip of paper.

"It looks as though things are heating up," he said, after scanning the document. "A Saudi Navy tug exiting Safaniya has been sunk by a mine. If there were any doubts about what those midgets were doing, I believe this confirms it."

Pickens bit his lower lip and nodded acquiescently.

"To answer your question, Mr. President," Lucerne continued, "it's time to move the Kitty Hawk Battle Group north and re-position our air assets. Further, we have already transmitted the coordinates of Iran's naval command center in Bushehr and several other key targets to the Annapolis. Once our forces are positioned I recommend giving Iran an ultimatum to return our midshipmen immediately and order their warships back to port. If they refuse, we take out their command center. If they still haven't gotten the message, we raise the ante by targeting the two Kilos. If they're foolish enough to put any aircraft up, we'll bring them down and destroy their airfields."

His no-nonsense response and iron gaze sent a nervous chill down Pickens' spine.

The room fell deadly silent while the president considered his options. Tiny beads of sweat appeared on his forehead and under the glow of the yellow map his face took on a jaundiced appearance.

Finally, looking up from his notes, he said without ceremony, "All of the above, general."

Chapter Fifteen

"That dumb sonofabitch," Dankworth complained to his second-in-command, who was seated nearby. "When the hell's he gonna figure it out? I've done every fuckin' thing but give the cretin a fuckin' road map. I knew Sampson was dense but I didn't think he was this stupid." His deep voice rose in anger, filling the sparsely furnished room.

Dankworth was anxiously pacing with the ferocity of a caged animal. The small room he'd selected for himself was located in the basement not far from the mids. No one was permitted to enter without being invited. It was his private domain and he made sure everyone understood that. As a rule, the former SEAL savored the comradeship of his men, extracting a sense of power from their dependence upon him. But he had his brooding moments and during those periods he needed solitude.

"Maybe he isn't as smart as you think, boss," the other man replied in his thick German accent. "After all, he's working with the feds and they ain't that swift."

Dankworth paused next to the makeshift table, pock-marked with rust but sturdy, and snatched his plastic cup, the large 24 ounce type used for slurpees. Lifting the cover of the styrofoam cooler, he scooped up a handful of ice then withdrew the chilled bottle of Absolut vodka, his drink of choice. It was almost noon and he was about to knock off the last of the quart. Pouring several ounces, he eyed the remaining few and emptied the bottle then tossed it into a nearby carton with the others. Despite the amount of booze in his system he appeared sober and lucid. Dankworth had one of those rare metabolisms that allowed him to consume vast amounts of alcohol without impairing his motor skills.

"Bullshit! He knows damn well. I've left enough clues to paint the Sistine Chapel," he groused, then drank thirstily. "Naw. That's not the problem," he mused.

The other man was tempted to ask, "So, what is the problem?" But he decided to remain discreetly quiet. He knew Bull wouldn't appreciate even the slightest hint that his well-thought out plan might be unravelling.

Shifting topics, Dankworth asked, "How are the squids holding up?"

Abruptly changing subjects was his way of resolving dilemmas for which he had no immediate solution. The temporary diversion allowed him to consign the problem to his subconscious while he focused on other issues.

"With the exception of that Lucerne whore, they've fallen into another slump," the German replied indifferently. "They've probably figured out Zablocki ain't coming back and they ain't taking it good. Morale's really low, despite her attempts to rally them."

"That's good," Dankworth retorted, removing another bottle from an open carton and plunging it into the ice chest. "That's the way I want `em. We don't need those shitheads getting brave and doing something stupid as we get down to the wire. We're going to have our hands full when Sampson and his boy scouts finally get around to finding us. If I didn't need them later I'd slit all their fuckin' candy-assed throats and feed `em to the fishes."

The notion excited the other man. "Let's cut up a few. We don't need all of them."

"Sometimes, I think you're sicker than me," Dankworth said, shaking his head. "Leave me alone for awhile. I gotta think."

* * *

Trish Mathews changed the lock on her apartment and willingly accepted a sensor alarm from Sampson after he'd failed to convince her to leave town for a few days, at least, he'd urged, until after the deadline. She refused, insisting she was committed to seeing the story to the end while asserting that if she were a target, as Sampson feared, they could easily have killed her that night at the Tidal Basin. She also argued forcefully against assigning someone to watch over her, insisting that the newspaper's offices provided ample security. Nor did she wish to do anything to curtail the flow of information that would ultimately find its way into her news story.

When the phone rang she picked it up without concern.

"Hi ya, baby."

This time, Dankworth's voice jarred her.

"Did you miss me?" He was arrogant and slurring his words.

"You sick piece of garbage," she hissed back at him. "Why don't you come out from under your rock instead of intimidating me this way? Do I frighten you?"

"Aren't you overreacting, doll face? I told you before, this is bigger than a few mids. Listen, we took more casualties in the first hours of the Persian Gulf War than this little op. Come on, get serious. Would you rather body bags start coming home from the gulf?"

He had a way of distracting her.

"I don't happen to agree with you," she countered, while trying to put a face to his voice. "First of all, there's no godly justification for what you've done."

He cut her off sharply, "Just a goddamned second, Trish! What the hell do you know about warfare? What depth of experience are you bringing to this party?"

His sudden outburst threw her and she mumbled, "Well...,

"You're nothing but a voyeur!" he continued angrily. "You stick your educated nose into other people's tragedies and write about their miserable lives and foolishly think because you've reported some personal tragedy that you're some kind of expert or you made some fucking contribution to humanity. What you're really doing is jumping from human tragedy to human tragedy like some fucking parasite, making a name for yourself at the expense of the people you're reporting about. For you, it's nothing more than an ego trip! And, when the going gets a little rough, what do you and your scumbag colleagues do? You run for cover, waving your First Amendment rights like a white flag on the battlefield. You don't have a fucking clue about what's going on in this screwed up world, Trish. The most dissonance you experience in your sterile, little world is when your editor cuts up your precious story or somebody slams a door in your face. You're kidding yourself if you think that writing a shallow news piece about base closures or some choreographed military exercise that's spelled out for you in some bullshit press release qualifies you to be a fucking expert on the military."

Trish was stunned. He'd touched a nerve when he criticized her for stroking her own ego. It was true. She and her colleagues derived great satisfaction from seeing their names rise like stars in the public arena. But they never openly admitted it. Occasionally, among themselves, they did. Usually when they felt secure in their jobs and had a wall filled with plaques and awards but certainly not to outsiders. They preferred thinking of themselves as the glue that held a democracy together. On the face of it, listening to him, she had to admit it was an ignoble attitude.

"You've never seen a shot fired in anger, Trish, but you're quick to judge me `cause I don't fit your fucking stereotypical concept of what a warrior should be. Nevertheless, sweetpea, I ain't afraid to die. My cause may be 180 degrees from yours right now, but at least I'm no fucking sponge, Trish. I'm no leech, pretending to care about what she reports, when all she's really interested in is her self-glorification! That all-important *by-line*. That's really the bottom line, ain't it, Trish?" he taunted. "You can be honest with me."

She held her tongue, noting, in criticizing her, he'd departed from his routine of keeping the conversation brief. He obviously didn't care this time that the call might be traced. She wondered what she could say to keep him talking.

As if reading her thoughts, he said, more calmly now, "I've talked long enough, darlin'. I didn't call just to lecture you. I want you to dig an article out of your vast library. You'll find it in the October 1977 issue of the *American Psychiatric Journal*."

"What's the title of the article?" she asked, as she wrote.

"How do you expect me to remember! Get the goddamn magazine and give it to Sampson," he instructed, before hanging up.

Sampson met her in the *Post's* lobby an hour later, where she handed him the publication. It was a single topic issue, devoted exclusively to psychiatric studies of Vietnam veterans.

"What do you make of it?" she puzzled.

Sampson shrugged as he scanned the index of titles, not knowing what he was looking for until he saw it.

"Here," he pointed. "This is what he wanted me to see."

The article, entitled, "Psychotic Warriors: the Joy of Killing," was based upon a series of studies conducted in VA hospitals with patients who had repeatedly volunteered for combat duty in Vietnam, in which many served several back-to-back tours in the most hostile regions, emerging from the war with little or no significant physical injuries.

"I'm afraid I don't understand, Tom. What is this going to tell you?"

"I don't know," he lied. "Perhaps after reading it I'll know better. I'd like to take it with me. Any problems?"

"No. None. Just return it when you've finished," she said casually. Then, taking his arm, she implored, "Please be careful. He's sick. I don't think he cares much about himself."

"He's sick alright," Sampson responded, icily. "But, there's no need to worry," he assured her. "I know how to handle him."

Sampson returned immediately to the Pentagon, phoning Cort along the way.

The two sat alone in the small office, the magazine face up on the desk between them.

"Bull's really pushing you," Cort said.

"Yeah. I figured he would," Sampson replied, calmly. "He wants my ass in his cross hairs big time. Once I knew it was him, I knew he'd get impatient when things didn't move according to his timetable."

"Bull may be a fruit cake, Duke, but he's a dangerous fruit cake. You'll have to watch your sixes all the way."

"Not to worry. I'm the hunter and he's the prey. You get your ass down to New Orleans asap. What time's your flight?"

Cort checked his Rolex, "Forty-five minutes."

Across the Potomac, at Andrews Air Force Base, a Navy T-39 was being fueled while the crew made preparations to take Cort to NAS New Orleans. The plane would wait for him as he searched the Navy's microfiche files of retired personnel. Somewhere in

Dankworth's service records was the clue he wanted Sampson to find that would bring the two SEALs face-to-face. Sampson knew it would be an encounter that would leave one and, quite possibly both men dead.

Chapter Sixteen

When Sampson's bedside phone rang at 12:15 he'd been asleep for over an hour. It was 11:15 in New Orleans.

He picked it up on the first ring. "Sampson," he said, fully awake.

"Cort, here. I've located Bull's service records. They're making a copy of everything as we speak." He sounded tired and irritable.

"Did you look at it?"

"No time. We've been searching for the damn thing for an hour and a half. This place is unbelievable. I don't think they've ever seen or heard of a computer. It's got to be the most archaic system in the world, everything's processed and filed by hand. And worse, none of the staff has ever heard of the word, *urgent*. It's a damn good thing I came down here or else we'd be retired before they got around to getting it to us. Since I don't know what I'm looking for, I decided to bring it all back rather than wasting time here."

"Good. How long you figure it'll take?" he asked, anxiously.

"Shit. A while. We're not talking high tech, here. If the damn copy machines don't break down, maybe another hour or two. That sonofabitch's file is huge."

"So, I should expect you around seven or so?"

"'Fraid so, boss. Where do you want to rendezvous? Your apartment?"

"No. Call me before you take off and I'll pick you up at Andrews. I want to examine his record at the command center."

"Roger. Talk to you later."

Sampson checked the time, turned off the light and went back to sleep.

A front had moved in during the night, pushing the previous day's clouds to sea and bringing with it a blast of Arctic air. As a result, early risers were greeted with the season's first lingering frost. Small puddles frozen over night glistened in the dazzling sun.

Cort's plane taxied to the hangar and stopped several yards away from Sampson's car. By 7:30 they were speeding east on Route 50 against the stream of Washington-bound commuters. The briefcase containing Dankworth's life history lay on the rear seat.

Across the river in Virginia, Trish stood stiffly in her parking lot. Buffeted by the morning wind, she fumbled with gloved hands to separate her car key from the others on the ring. Her progress was hampered by bits of grit whipped up into her face. Putting the wind to her back, she squinted through a veil of hair and mumbled a string of curses until finally popping the door open. She jumped in and instantly regretted not zipping the wool liner into her Burberrys raincoat. The smooth, leather seats were ice cold. Anxious for heat, she stabbed the key into the ignition and pressed hard against the accelerator. With the engine coughing and spurting she pumped the pedal while clearing the frosty crust from the windshield with her wipers. Then, shifting into drive, she inched out of the shadows to a spot where the sun shone. With the warm rays hitting her face, she turned on the radio, closed her eyes and leaned back. Soon the engine was running smoothly and she grasped the mirror, twisted it and began brushing her hair from her face. Moving closer to check her mascara, she caught sight of the white plastic bag on the rear seat. Startled, she turned and stared at it. She knew it wasn't hers, nor was it there when she parked the previous evening.

Now, with her pulse racing she took a hasty inventory and determined nothing was missing - not the loose change in the receptacle below the radio, nor the cassette tapes strewn on the passenger's seat. She pressed her memory to recall if she had left the car unlocked, then quickly dismissed the notion since she had found it locked. She looked back again at the parcel, only faintly aware of the stream of dialogue from the two morning disc jockeys. Should she reach back and pick it up? She knew she didn't have to open it to know the contents would be unsettling.

Finally, when her curiosity overcame her fear, she leaned over and, with a trembling hand, picked it up.

It was 8:30 when Sampson and Cort entered the command center. The level of activity was greater than usual.

"What's going on?" Sampson asked the duty officer.

"We got a call twenty-five minutes ago, commander. The news reporter from the *Post*, the one who's been the point of contact. She found a package in her car this morning. A video tape. She took it back to her apartment and played it. Pretty messy stuff from the way she described it. She asked for you and I told her you hadn't arrived yet. I dispatched someone from the Pentagon to her apartment. They've already retrieved the tape and made a copy for General Lucerne. They're on their way here with it, now. If they don't hit any traffic, it should arrive within the hour."

"Where is she now?" Sampson's anger swelled as he thought of what Dankworth was putting her through.

"She waited for our man then left with him. She said to tell you she was on her way to Senator Bennett's home and would call you later. The note attached to the package said a copy of the tape had also been delivered to the Bennett's. This guy's creating a lot of turmoil," the duty officer said, mournfully.

"Yeah. And it ain't going to get any better. Let me know when it arrives."

"Aye, aye, sir."

"The asshole's having a good time," Cort said.

"He damn well better enjoy himself now," Sampson scowled, "because when I catch the bastard it'll all be over. Let's get started on his service record."

"How bad was it, John?" Hemmings asked Lucerne, sensing his pain.

"Bad," came the reply. There was no mistaking his controlled anger. "I'm not going to allow Miriam to see it. It would serve no useful purpose and only sicken her more. Unfortunately, Bennett's wife found the damn thing wrapped in the morning newspaper. The kids have been roughed up and abused, some worse than others. They forced them to read the latest demands on camera. Bastards."

"How did Ingrid look?" Hemmings asked with concern.

"They didn't show her or the Bennett boy."

For the first time since the incident began, Hemmings noted that his friend sounded weary.

"Nothing like psychological warfare to wear the troops down," Hemmings commented. "You're supposed to extrapolate from their absence that they're either worse off or...," He paused but Lucerne quickly completed the painful thought.

"...Or dead," he said, coldly.   "They're keeping us on tenterhooks down to the wire so we don't push the president in the wrong direction, Ray. Boy, I'd love to get my hands on them."

Lucerne had called Hemmings soon after viewing the tape. Though the visuals were loathsome, it was the message which concerned him most and with which he, as acting Chairman, had to deal.

"A copy's on its way to you," he told the Director. "They've raised the ante and we'll need to meet with Pickens to discuss it."

"How will it affect our plans?" Hemmings asked.

"Despite the added pressure, which I suspect Bennett is undoubtedly applying at this very moment," Lucerne replied, confidently, "I don't think we'll have to alter them much, if at all."

Meanwhile, at the White House, Pickens was forced to cancel an early morning staff meeting to accommodate Bennett, who had called immediately after viewing the video and calming his wife. He arrived at the White House alone twenty minutes later hunting for bear.

Tossing the tape unceremoniously at McCurdy, who had escorted him into the president's office, he ordered, "Put that on." He then sat down, glowering at Pickens as the five minute drama played out.

"Jesus, Mary and Saint Joseph," Pickens exclaimed with a grimace when it ended.

"They ain't going to help them, Les. Not on this earth. Maybe in the next world, which is what I've been asking you to avoid since this damn thing started. Does this finally convince you of the urgency to do something that will deliver those poor kids back to us in one piece? Aren't their precious lives worth more than a bunch of A-rabs?" he said, intentionally mispronouncing the final word to emphasize his disdain.

The images of their battered and swollen faces left Pickens badly shaken. "I didn't see your boy, Russ," he offered, hinting his absence might suggest he may not have been harmed beyond the loss of his finger.

"Exactly, Les," he responded, wearily. "They want to leave me in the dark about his condition. At least we know those mids," he said, pointing a shaking finger at the blank screen, "are still alive. Beaten, but alive, Les. Why didn't they put Russ on camera? Has he already been murdered, too badly beaten or will he be the next to go if we don't abide by their demands?"

For the next twenty minutes Bennett first pleaded then cajoled and finally threatened Pickens with political annihilation if he didn't secure his son's safe release.

Throughout the tirade the president nodded sympathetically but wisely offered nothing concrete, except to advise his friend that the situation in the gulf had deteriorated to the point that he couldn't allow America to stand idly by.

When pressed by Bennett, he asked McCurdy to brief the senator on the NSC's interpretation of Iran's intentions based upon the most recent intelligence reports and analyses.

"You believe that bullshit?" Bennett retorted, in a last desperate bid after hearing the summary. "Can't you see that's Lucerne's way of getting you to support his position? You can't believe for a moment Iran would try anything so foolish," he argued. "They'd never get away with it! The international community would come down all over them. Can't you see they're only trying to keep the Saudis contained while they strike Iraq? Because a lousy Saudi tug hits a mine we're supposed to believe they intend to invade Saudi Arabia. Shit, Les, ships have been hitting mines in those waters for years. They're all over the damn place. How can you allow yourself to be taken in by such bellicose nonsense? And, those accusations by the Fundamentalists..., pure vitriolic rhetoric! Nothing more, Les.

135

They've been spewing that bullshit since ousting the Shah. Why should we give it anymore credence now? Don't be fooled by Lucerne and his cronies," he admonished. "You've got to do what they ask in this latest communique." He stood before Pickens pointing to the television.

This time his badgering produced only vague assurances from the overwrought president, who promised to do whatever possible to secure the safe release of his son after taking this latest development under advisement.

The two men parted not happily.

At Lucerne's urging, Diamond had convinced the beleaguered Pickens that the latest Iranian missive didn't require a full blown NSC meeting. Diamond assured the deteriorating president that the latest round of demands could be addressed by the principals alone as they'd done in his office before. It was the only good news he'd heard that morning. After the ordeal with Bennett, he accepted the recommendation without argument.

The meeting moved quickly, with Lucerne assuring Pickens, to his great relief, that the demands mouthed by the frightened mids on the tape could be met easily without changing the action they had agreed to take earlier.

"They're a little slow on the uptake, Mr. President," Lucerne said. "Moving our spy satellite orbits away from the gulf isn't a problem at this juncture. We aren't going to gain much more by keeping them there than we don't already know. The most important data - the target coordinates for calibrating our Tomahawks - have already been gathered. Let's accommodate them. If we need anything later on, we can send up the SR-71s."

"As for assuring them that Israel won't step in," Diamond said, "we'll simply tell them Israel has agreed."

"But, they haven't," Pickens replied, nervously.

"Mr. President," Hemmings volunteered, "it doesn't matter. Israel won't do anything without first obtaining our concurrence. But, it will never reach that stage because we're going to stop them before they get started."

Hemmings' certitude had a visibly calming affect on the president, who'd been drinking nervously from his mug since they entered his office.

"And the money? What about their frozen assets?"

They all noticed the emerging twitch below his left eye.

Harrison spoke up first. "I think we should tell them we'll deposit it in, say, Switzerland. Once the mids are released we'll release it."

"That's a wise course," Hemmings inserted. "We can't be seen jumping at every demand. It would be out of character."

"And their insistence that the UN Security Council won't come out against them? What about that?" Pickens seemed no longer capable of offering solutions.

"That's easy, sir," Harrison reassured him. "Our UN ambassador will guarantee them that we will veto any such attempts. We've never dealt with the Iranians on this level before, so there's no reason to expect they won't believe us."

"Besides, Mr. President," Hemmings interrupted, "this last demand is a sop. They don't really care what happens in New York after they've taken over the oil fields. They're rubbing our faces in it," he added, contemptuously, "because they think they have us over a barrel."

"Well, they do, in a sense," Pickens said, perspiration clinging to his brow. He was still smarting from his bout with Bennett. "They've got our midshipmen." The words no sooner left his mouth than he regretted saying them, conscious of Lucerne's silent gaze. "What I mean is, we can't act in total disregard of their safety. I'm sure you would agree."

The room fell silent for an agonizing moment until Lucerne came to his rescue. "We're working that problem and we're making progress," he said, noncommittally.

"What progress?" Pickens leapt on the statement.

"It's preliminary, Mr. President, but we may have something very soon. Sampson is certain they're onto something that will lead us to them. I regret that's all we have at the moment but the situation may change abruptly."

Despite its vagueness, this latest bit of information had a decidedly uplifting affect on Pickens and, for the first time he smiled.

Chapter Seventeen

It didn't take Sampson long to ferret out the clue Dankworth had set him up to find. His service record was a mosaic of evaluations, medals, awards, commendations and veiled notes of censure going back to his early Navy days. Most of the information confirmed what Sampson already knew of the fallen warrior. The portrait that emerged from twenty-eight years of military service was as enigmatic as the man, who rallied his troops in combat while clashing with the bureaucracy. Sampson thought that in another time, perhaps the middle ages, when warriors reigned supreme, he would have likely earned himself a place in history, perhaps even a noble one.

Dankworth hadn't become aggressive in the Navy, he came to it that way. Given the option of jail for grand larceny in his hometown of Fairfield, Connecticut or enlisting on the first day of his seventeenth year, he chose the latter. Boot camp discipline didn't diminish his combative spirit, it simply re-channelled it. Winning honors in boxing and wrestling competitions advanced his class standing and allowed him to select his first duty station after graduation, a rare perk for most recruits. Like a moth drawn to a flame, he alone, in a class of 400 volunteered for duty with American advisors operating patrol boats in South Vietnam's hostile Mekong Delta. It was an extremely unusual request, Sampson mused, considering the U. S. had not yet been drawn into the conflict.

Commendations citing his bravery and tactical acuity in combat were numerous and promotions came rapidly. After two back-to-back tours in-country, interrupted by only a six month stint at the Amphibious Training School in Coronado, California, which included combat training with the Marines, he was promoted to boatswain second class and sported more ribbons on his uniform than most senior enlisted men and officers under whom he served. His brief career at that point had been dominated in one way or another by combat at a time when battle-proven veterans were in high demand. Thereafter, with a few minor exceptions - when there wasn't a war to fight - he was training for one. And, it was those exceptions that gave Sampson the information he sought.

"Do you see the pattern?" he asked Cort, as they passed pages from Dankworth's service record between them.

"If you mean, he's a war nut, yeah. The guy can't stay away from it. He's seen more combat than anyone I know. Look at his kill record! It's incredible. Almost like a sexual thing."

"No, not that. Look at where he's served," Sampson replied.

"So? He's a PacFleet sailor. What of it? It's not unusual to spend an entire career in the Pacific. The Pentagon's loaded with senior officers who had to be yanked back to Washington from the fleet for that obligatory Washington tour prior to making flag. Who else but bean counters and bureaucrats would get their rocks off in that puzzle palace?"

"Under ordinary circumstances," Sampson agreed, "it wouldn't amount to anything. But, we're not looking for an ordinary sailor. Check those duty stations," he said, handing him the list.

Cort read down the list then shook his head. "I'm looking but I don't see a pattern."

"Dankworth's had only a few east coast tours," Sampson pointed out. "The first was when he entered the Navy through Recruit Training Center, in Bainbridge. The second, involved instructor duty at the Naval Academy and the College Preparatory School, also located at Bainbridge."

"Hold it!" Cort interrupted as he shuffled through several pages. "I saw something..., Wait. Here it is. He went to Captain's Mast during that tour and was awarded a reduction in rank and a letter of reprimand. His tour was cut short after fourteen months and he was returned to the fleet."

"What did he do?" Sampson asked.

"Says here, he verbally abused students and applied excessive force against several of them during physical training. Sounds like he took a bunch of them on and beat the shit out of them."

"Looks like that was the beginning of his love-hate relationship with the academy," Sampson reflected. "Yet, it didn't stop his star from rising. His third east coast stint was Officer Candidate School at Newport, Rhode Island, followed by orders to SEAL school in San Diego," he read aloud. "His fourth trip back here was to Perry Point VA hospital where he underwent psychiatric evaluation after three consecutive tours in Vietnam and Cambodia."

"Yeah. Got it right here," Cort said, turning to Dankworth's medical history. "Eight months at Point Perry." Scanning it, he said, "This is strange. Bull's medical record was amended in 1983, nine years after he was treated. According to this letter, signed by the Surgeon General, the original evaluator, a civilian doctor with ties to anti-war movements was deemed unduly harsh and lacked medical objectivity in appraising Dankworth's performance under combat. It says, that after a board of certified psychiatrists reviewed Bull's medical history, the file was corrected and the earlier evaluation was expunged. There's no further mention of his treatment at Perry Point other than describing it as recuperative. They gave him a clean bill of health. Looks like he had friends in high places who didn't want to see his combat record marred."

"Particularly at promotion time," Sampson commented bitterly. "It's nice having such friends," he added, as he spit into the empty coke can.

"1983? Wasn't that just after he was called back to establish Red Cell?" Cort noted.

"Yeah. He was scheduled to appear before some congressional committees to explain how he intended to spend the black program money. The brass probably wanted to be certain he was squeaky clean in case some disgruntled congressman decided to torpedo the operation," Sampson said. "But let's not get side tracked. What do you draw from those tours of duty?"

"He managed to keep as far away from Washington politics as possible and I don't blame him."

Sampson walked to the wall map. "Look," he said, pointing to the area just north of Baltimore. "Here's Bainbridge and here's Perry Point. They're about five miles apart and fifty miles from Annapolis. Our friend has spent three of his five east coast tours in this triangle. We're looking for a guy who kidnaps ten mids in the middle of the day and has to hide them quickly and safely. We haven't been able to find him because up to now we've been looking west, toward the Blue Ridge mountains, figuring there are thousands of square miles of national parks in which to hide. Dankworth's never been to those parks and doesn't know shit about them. In fact, you look at his life and, outside of Washington and Fairfield, he wouldn't know much at all about the east coast - with this one exception."

"Damn!" Cort said. "It's so obvious. That's how the sonofabitch gets to Trish so easily. He comes down at night, does his shit and he's back under his rock before sunrise. Incredible."

Sampson was already thinking of other matters. "Let's see," he muttered while studying the map, "As I recall, we shut that place down in the mid-seventies," he said of the training center. "I'll bet we still own it."

Cort was focusing on the surrounding area. "It's one helluva handy location. Less than an hour from Annapolis and less than two from the District. And look at the airports at his disposal..., Dulles, BWI, Philadelphia and JFK. That's probably where the fingers were moved out of."

"And Valerius, too," Sampson added sourly.

There was a knock on the door and the duty officer entered. "Commander," he said, "the video tape's here. It's in the machine and ready to go as soon as the Supe arrives, which should be very soon. Would you like to preview it or wait for him?"

"I'll wait, thanks," he said, reaching for the academy phone book. Pressing it open with his elbow, he cradled the phone on his shoulder, dialed and waited.

"This is Commander Tom Sampson. May I speak with Commander Barone? Sure, I'll wait." He winked at Cort. "NavFac officer," he said, before turning back to the phone. "Hello, Frank. I'm okay but I can't talk right now. I need some info fast. Do we still own Bainbridge? Uh uh. Good. Who's it come under? Thanks, pal. Talk to you soon."

He hung up, then said, "The clock's running, buddy. Get your ass down to the Navy Yard, pronto. Go to NavFac. The admiral's

office. I'll give `em a head's up. Get all you can on Bainbridge...,
aerial maps, schematics, blue prints, perimeter roads, train and
port facilities, utility charts for gas, phone, power lines, water and
sewage lines, history..., everything Naval Facilities has."

Next, he had the duty officer page his team, instructing them
to return to the command center asap while he placed a call to the
Navy Command Center in the Pentagon. He was winding up the
last call just as Harding arrived.

The small briefing room had only fifteen seats and all were
taken. The overflow stood silently along the rear wall watching
the video. The lights were dimmed and they watched somberly as
each battered midshipman appeared before them and delivered
Iran's latest demands. When the tape had played through the room
was charged with indignation but no one spoke. All eyes fell to
Harding in the front row.

"That was brutal," he said with obvious disgust. His hands
were balled into tight fists. "I can't believe the bastard is one of
us. He'll pay for this."

"Admiral," Sampson whispered, "we need to talk privately."

Harding turned. His mind was clearly elsewhere. "What,
Tom? What'd you say?"

"I have some positive information to report," he said, quietly.
"Something that needs to be discussed in private, sir."

"Of course, Tom. Let's go to your office."

They walked down the hall in silence. Inside, Sampson closed
the door and offered the admiral his chair.

"There's something I haven't told you about this operation. I
believe Dankworth has made this a personal vendetta between us
which he intends to conclude on the field of battle."

"What?" Harding said, in disbelief. "How did you figure that
out?"

"Actually, I've suspected it for a while. He wants to kill me, I
believe even at the risk of jeopardizing this op. It sounds crazy but
I know he's setting me up. I'm sure he thinks he can outwit me. It
goes back to his court martial, for which he blames me."

Harding shook his head. "It seems this whole operation is providing him the means of settling a lot of old scores. It's diabolical."

"Yep. Including his targeting the mids, as I'm about to show you. Our former shipmate has provided the clue that will take us to him."

"Jesus. This gets more bizarre every day."

Harding listened in rapt silence as Sampson walked him through Dankworth's service history.

Harding let out a long sigh when Sampson had finished. Fatigue lines crisscrossed his face. Nothing in his long Navy career had prepared him for this and he was quick to admit it. "If you're right..., He's a formidable enemy..., I don't feel good about getting our mids out safely," he confessed. "How do you suggest we proceed?"

"For openers, I'd like to keep what I've told you under wraps for the next twenty-four hours while my men and I conduct a recon of the area. If we're going to be drawn into his web, I'd like to at least maintain the element of surprise. It'll be critical when we go in."

"You afraid of leaks, Tom?"

"Let me put it this way, admiral. Dankworth never puts an op together without first establishing an intel network."

The notion surprised Harding and he asked, "You think he's got collaborators working inside?"

"It's possible, but I doubt it. Yet, we are being observed. You can be certain of that. And, since he's luring us to him, I want to avoid sending any signals that might reveal how much we know or our intentions. While I trust those around us..., As they used to say, `A slip of the lip' could do us in. Just give me and my men enough time to develop a plan of attack. We can expand the players as necessary when the time comes."

"Certainly," he said without hesitation. "We've got to overpower him and his soldiers before they can move against their hostages. You and your men are the most qualified to carry out that mission."

When Harding stood to leave, there was a momentary unsteadiness making him look older and more frail than he had been just a week earlier. Sampson pretended not to notice.

With his hand on the knob, Harding turned and said before leaving, "Be extremely careful, commander."

"Aye, aye, sir," the SEAL replied smartly.

Cort was back by noon toting a briefcase crammed with information.

"If he's there, as you suspect, we got our work cut out," he offered while heaving the briefcase onto the desk. "It's a big area, over 1,200 acres in the middle of nowhere. He's isolated himself in wilderness."

"I'm not surprised," Sampson responded. "It's ideal for his purpose. He's probably layered himself with perimeter security, too," he added, his mind already working the problem. Since determining Bull was at Bainbridge, he hadn't stopped thinking of what it would take to outsmart his former shipmate and affect a successful rescue.

Cort, busily placing the material on the desk, added, "No doubt, with Iran's funding he'll have a well-equipped team."

The phone rang and Sampson picked it up. "Commander Sampson. Yes. Fine. Forty-five minutes?" He checked his watch and said, "Excellent. See you then. That was Lucerne's office," he told Cort. "He's arranged for an unmarked helo to pick me up. I'm going to do an aerial recon. Did you get a map?"

Cort withdrew and unfolded a three by four-foot development map of the complex from several in a pile. Spreading it out on a table, he said, "This is the most recent one on file. It's dated October 1962, reflecting the training center at its height. Its the one our engineers used two years ago when they started dismantling the place."

"What? You mean there aren't any buildings on the site?" Sampson asked with alarm, knowing Dankworth would need protection from the weather and curious eyes. Establishing a hideout in the center of vacant property made no sense. Sampson had assumed, when he identified Bainbridge as Dankworth's sanctuary, that there were abandoned structures from which the ex-SEAL would have to be extracted. If the old buildings had been torn down, then he had flawed in his reasoning and had wasted valuable time misreading his service record.

"Slow down." Cort cautioned, grasping Sampson's concerns. "You're getting ahead of yourself. The place hasn't been completely razed. In a nutshell, the training center was built around property the Navy bought in 1942 from the Jacob Tome Institute, a boys' prep school built in 1900 by Jacob Tome, a local wealthy logger by trade. When we entered World War II, we needed a place to train recruits and, coincidentally, the prep school was up for sale. We took it over, expanding it from the original 350 acres to 1,200 acres for our boot camp and other schools until closing it down in June 1976. That's when we turned it over to the Labor Department, which used it from 1978-1990 as a Job Corps Center. What those misfits didn't destroy, they stole. After that, the Navy declared the real estate excess and offered it to Maryland. Before transferring it, we had to absorb the cost of clearing the land and returning it to its natural state. That meant tearing down the buildings and ripping up the old railroad tracks we installed over the years. "But, not," he quickly added as he pointed to the lower left hand section of the map, "the prep school and its surrounding buildings, located down here in this sector. They're still standing," he explained, "because they're on the national register of historic buildings."

"So, who has control of the land, the Navy or Maryland?" Sampson asked.

"It's in limbo, somewhere between the federal government and the state, working its way through the maze of paperwork. God knows how long that'll take. In the meantime, it sits there posted with no trespassing signs, fenced off from the rest of the world. Convenient, eh?"

Sampson looked at his watch. "Good job, shipmate. The team should be assembling soon. Get everyone up to speed on the terrain. I'll be back before you've finished. Oh, yeah. Lay on hourly FLIR flights beginning at seven tonight."

Twenty minutes later, Sampson's helo lifted off from the academy's lacrosse field and headed north along the narrowing

Chesapeake, to the mouth of the Susquehanna River. During the brief flight he studied the NavFac map spread across his lap.

The civilian-painted helo, one of several unmarked aircraft in the Secret Service's inventory, was equipped with powerful, gyro-stabilized binoculars that enabled Sampson to easily survey every square meter of the desolate base without having to fly directly over it. The sky was clear and the November sun shone brilliantly on the rolling hills below. From the air, Bainbridge was easily identifiable. Its triangular shape was defined by wide county roads flanking its eastern and western perimeters which vectored from the small enclave of Port Deposit along the rambling Susquehanna at its southern base and converged into an inverted V to the north.

Sampson didn't need the map to distinguish the prep school buildings, grouped in the lower portion of the sprawling base. They stood out from a handful of smaller, one and two story structures scattered in an arc, nearby. As the helo crisscrossed the barren farmlands and small towns of Maryland's Cecil and Harford counties in the upper most northeastern sector of the state, he made extensive notations on his map and accompanying notebook while the two rear passengers used their expert skills to cover every aspect of the target area and surrounding countryside with still and video cameras. After twenty-five minutes, assured by the photographers that they had captured as much as possible from the air, Sampson instructed the pilot to land.

They set down on the grassy knoll, fronting the admin building at Perry Point. A Secret Service agent driving a metallic gray Jeep Cherokee, its windows tinted and bearing Maryland plates was waiting for them. Sampson jumped out and went immediately to the Veterans Administration security officer and thanked him for his support while the two photographers transferred their equipment to the jeep. Minutes later they were heading out the main gate, past the small police shack back toward Bainbridge, 4.5 miles away on state route 222.

The driver was a pro and held to just below the speed limit while circling the sprawling, seemingly deserted complex. If Dankworth's men were guarding the perimeter fence, as Sampson suspected, he'd be limited to one pass without being detected. There would be other observers at various times throughout the night and the following day in an array of different vehicles but for now, one pass was all they were willing to risk. It was difficult, and in some instances impossible, seeing beyond the dense oaks and scrub pines that grew flush with the hurricane fence. But that changed when they reached the former main entrance to the base, where the red brick foundation and mounted, concrete signboard stood at the intersection. The driver entered and passed through two large parking lots to the padlocked main gate. The view through the gate was unobstructed but there wasn't much to see. From outside the gate the base resembled a ghost town. The main street, which Sampson identified on the map as Bainbridge Road, was badly cracked and weather worn and overgrown with dry weeds and shrubs. They could see down it for several hundred yards before it rose and swerved to the left and disappeared in the distance. Rather than stop, the driver approached the gate slowly then made a U-turn and returned to the main road. As they re-entered the state road, Sampson noticed the trees around the entrance had been thinned out. He also saw a silhouette in the window of the former caretaker's two story house abutting the road.

Back at the intersection, they turned right toward Port Deposit. The road quickly fell away from the base, curving sharply as it descended precipitously toward the town and the adjoining river. It was an unusual town, only three or four blocks long, depending on which side of the street one walked. The structures were permanently locked between the steep granite cliffs that formed the base of the training center and the rail bed that paralleled the broad mouth of the rushing Susquehanna. Quite simply, it was prevented by nature from growing any larger than it already had. Sampson and the others hadn't seen anything like it. It consisted of only two rows of buildings divided by the narrow main street, which could become narrower still, when encountering a parked car. Most of the riverside structures were modest dwellings and occasional shops and a restaurant and bar that seemed to be the town's only diversion. The buildings on the cliff side were larger or, so it appeared. Probably, Sampson surmised, because they were constructed above the road, on excavated portions of the cliff. There was an equal number of smaller clapboard houses interspersed among them. All seemed to be built around the turn of the century and all retained the dirt and soot of an industrial town. As they drove, they passed a municipal building, a library and a combination post office and police station. Then, suddenly, they were out of the town.

They made a U-turn where the narrow road inexplicably widened for a short distance and returned to state route 276, the only other road into town. There, they turned left and climbed to the summit. At the top, the government posted, hurricane fence resumed. This portion of the perimeter was the straightest and longest leg, measuring 1.9 miles. Free of foliage to accommodate the nine padlocked gates and the double gauge rail spur, it provided an unobstructed view of the western edge of the base. Unfortunately, there wasn't much to see. According to Sampson's map that area had at one time been the site of two large drill fields and numerous barracks, all of which, he had noted from the helo, were now demolished and the rubble removed. Most of the terrain was flat, providing a distinct advantage to those defending it.

* * *

Phase two began shortly after Sampson's helo deposited him back in Annapolis and he met with his team.

"They've all seen the video tape," Cort notified him, "and we've got an excellent handle on the physical plant. But, there's something I want you to see before we get into that."

Sampson followed his assistant into the briefing theater where Cort turned on the video and instructed, "Look at the background, Tom." After it played through, he said, "The concrete floor and walls, the overhead pipes..., it was filmed in the basement of one of the Tome school buildings. That's where he's holding them."

"Makes sense," Sampson replied. "It has to be more secure than any of those few remaining frame buildings I saw beyond the prep schools. But how can you be certain?"

Cort gave him a broad smile and said, "This way."

They walked into one of the offices ringing the main command center. In the brief time during Sampson's absence, Cort had pored through the data from NavFac and sorted it while collecting additional data. By now the walls of the room were plastered with detailed maps and charts. There were federal, state and county maps highlighting main and secondary roadways, diagrams of utility trunk lines running through the region, topography, weather, oceanographic and air controller charts, lists of FCC radio frequencies used by the Army at nearby Aberdeen Proving Grounds as well as state, county and local police and fire department frequencies. Secured to a portable easel were listings of tide tables for the northern end of the Chesapeake, Conrail schedules and Maryland Department of Highways vehicular traffic analyses. The room was a beehive of activity as SEALs arrived with additional data from other sources while men combed through what had already been gathered.

Seated at a metal desk in the center of the room with a large magnifying glass was an elderly man. He was hunched over a schematic and oblivious to the upheaval around him.

"Excuse me, Dutch, I'd like you to meet Commander Tom Sampson, the man heading this operation," Cort said. "Commander, I'd like to introduce Dutch Schultz."

The old man sprang to his feet. He was as thin as a reed and he had a ruddy, outdoor complexion and a full head of cropped white hair. Sampson guessed he was in his mid-seventies. The manner in which he remained standing - almost at attention - suggested a military background.

"Pleased to meet you, Mr. Schultz," he said, grasping the outstretched hand.

He was corrected immediately by an overly loud, raspy voice. "Everyone calls me chief," Schultz shouted, a sparkle in his eyes. "Retired Chief Boiler Tender. Thirty-five years with Uncle Sam," he announced proudly, omitting all personal pronouns.

"It's an honor, chief." Sampson shouted back, aware that old timers like Schultz, who had spent their careers in noisy engine rooms often suffered hearing loss.

"The chief," Cort quickly pointed out with a raised voice, "was the caretaker at Bainbridge until December 1993. That's when they finished the demolition phase and closed it up in preparation to handing the place over to the state."

"Hated to see the old place close. Went through boot camp there in `43 and came back as caretaker in `79, shortly after hanging up the uniform. Know every square foot. Was born and raised in Kilby Corner, just four miles west. Used to sneak in and swim in the old reservoir before the Navy took over," he reflected with a smile. "Understand you got some trouble up there. Wanna be of assistance."

"He's been briefed on the situation," Cort volunteered. "I've also explained the problem with security and the chief understands he won't be leaving here until the op goes down."

Sampson looked at Schultz for confirmation.

"Yes, sir, commander. Here for the duration."

"Good. Welcome aboard, chief. We'll start the briefings as soon as I get the photography from my trip. No doubt your input will be valuable."

"Nasty business. World sure has changed for the worst," he shook his head solemnly. "Hope those mids can be saved."

"We're going to do our best," Sampson assured him.

"By the way," Schultz said as the two men started to leave, "All those buildings are connected by underground utility tunnels. Will point `em out on the map when you're ready."

"Count on it," Sampson said with a smile.

Schultz returned to his document, making a mental note to tell them about the snakes.

* * *

At nine that evening, the Bell 412-SP, a four-blade, twin engine helo, lifted off from Aberdeen's airfield for the first of its hourly night flights over Bainbridge, nine miles to the northwest. The pilot, a member of the U. S. Park Police, was on loan, this time to the Navy, a procedure he was well acquainted with since joining the force five years earlier. Nearly half of his flight time had been in support of the Secret Service and Defense Department, moving VIPs around and providing additional security with his airborne platform. Tonight he'd be circling the perimeter of the base at 1,500 feet, throttling back to reduce engine noise while his two passengers studied the ground through a monitor connected to the Forward Looking InfraRed camera mounted on the belly of the craft. The night was cold and crisp, further accentuating the images displayed on the monochrome screen.

Fifteen minutes later they were back on the ground with a clearer assessment of where Dankworth's men were deployed and the routes they used to get there. Of the eight main structures comprising the Tome Institute, they identified two emitting considerable temperature variations, a good indication they were occupied by more than a few people. Subsequent flights would substantiate which of the two was Dankworth's headquarters.

The flights continued unabated throughout the night, providing imagery that peeled away the layers of secrecy from Dankworth's headquarters and Sampson with valuable intelligence about his enemy. The pattern of contrasting heat traces soon revealed that Dankworth and his men were operating out of the largest building in the southwest corner of the base. Flanked by the palisades on one side, thin foliage along state route 276 on his west, the long driveway and expansive parking lot on his east, Dankworth had wisely isolated himself. From there, he could disperse his small army around the prep school's original 350 acre site with maximum effectiveness. Trails of heat across the monitor suggested he was using the remaining 900 acres as a buffer. The cameras picked up small roving bands of men during their periodic patrols. The observers noted with interest that they rarely ventured off the old road grid. The difficulty, Sampson perceived as he analyzed each new piece of data, would not be in penetrating the base but in rapidly piercing Dankworth's inner perimeter and reaching the mids before he or his men could take retribution against them.

The SEALs worked throughout the night, fueled by coffee, cold sandwiches and chewing tobacco. By early morning, as the sun broke over the eastern shore, they had completed a preliminary attack plan.

"Let's review it one more time," Sampson said to the sea of red eyes around him. "But first, I want to remind all of you, not just those who've heard of Bull Dankworth's exploits and accomplishments..., he's not superman. Admittedly, he knows our business as well as all of us. Hell," he said, unabashedly, "he invented many of our tactics. But, he's one man and he can only be in one place. Compared to you, the others on his team are all young recruits. Dankworth might correctly anticipate our assault against him, but that's not going to help his men. I don't give a damn who's trained them or where they've been trained - Syria, Libya or wherever. They're no match for us! And, most important, we'll still have the element of surprise. Remember that if you start seeing images of big, bad Bull flash before you." He noted with some concern when he'd finished that their somber expressions hadn't changed. Nodding to Cort, he said, "It's yours."

"All right, then," Cort began, "there aren't any original blue prints. None existed when we bought the place but there was a set made for the school by an early insurance survey. NavFac's searching their archives and, with any luck, they'll be here this afternoon. In the meantime, we got eight main buildings located around a large, uncultivated grass quadrangle and five outlying structures. The eight Tome buildings were constructed around 1900. The exterior walls are sawed granite. The roofs are slate. They can take a direct hit without sustaining much damage. The others, out beyond the school," he indicated their location on the map with a pointer, "were built by the Navy and are made of cement-asbestos board. Those, according to Chief Schultz," he said with a nod to the aged veteran, who was clearly enjoying his role in this phase of the operation, "you can put your fist through the walls."

As Cort spoke he moved between the map to his left and the enlarged color photos taken during Sampson's aerial recon and which were now taped to the wall to his right. They depicted boarded up structures, some covered with ivy, and all in various states of disrepair. The quality of the photography was so good that it was possible to read the signs posted above the entrances, declaring the buildings condemned and forbidding trespassing.

Placing his pointer on the large map, he said, "These 300 acres are our target. The area's located 200 feet atop the palisades on the north side of the Susquehanna, directly above Port Deposit and four miles east of the Conowingo Dam. The surrounding countryside is relatively flat, with no steep climbs. The river's a half mile wide and 14 feet deep alongside the city dock."

"What're we doing about the townfolks?" asked the SEAL who would be spending that day strolling the streets and taking lunch in the bar.

"It's a problem," Sampson interjected. "Since the town abuts the base we can't do anything that'll tip Dankworth off, like evacuating them or moving troops in. We'll have to work around them and try to limit the action to the base."

"Here's where we believe the mids are being held." Cort indicated a rectangular building designated, 1, which he had circled in red and highlighted. "It's the same one Bull's operating out of. You can see it clearly in these photos." His pointer touched the long, two storied structure. The main entrance was dominated by a classical portico of four Ionic granite columns. "It's seven hundred feet west of U. S. route 222 and sixteen hundred feet east of state route 276, here. Now, you all need to know the other aspects of this terrain. Notice the building across from building one. It's got a twelve-foot, four-sided clock tower mounted on top of it. Perfect for snipers. Next, the reservoir. It's at the high point of ground, abutting 276. I also want you to take note of the 36-inch sewage outfall pipe a quarter mile up 222. Midway between the reservoir and the school is the old power house," he said, locating its placement on the chart. "Everyone's met Chief Schultz. He'll talk to that. You're on, chief."

Schultz nodded and waited a moment as the SEALs turned to face him. "Power house was closed down in the fifties after the Navy built a larger one. Still there though, just like it was. Made from stones taken out of the quarry up the road. A stone lined tunnel, seven feet high by five feet wide, at an average underground depth of 10-15 feet goes from the power house in the direction of the buildings and branches off to each one. Was built to carry lagged steam and electricity lines into the basements of each building." He paused, anticipating questions.

"Ever been down there, chief?" one SEAL asked.

"Sure. But not recently. Doubt if anything's changed though."

"Are they dry? Much room to maneuver? What about the doors into the power house and the basements?"

"Made a walk-through inspection the summer of `92 during the final demolition phase. Plenty of rain that year but the tunnels were bone dry. As far as the power house doors go..., two thick wooden ones, covered with steel. Fire protection, you know. One on the north side, other on the south. Locks are nothing special - hasps with standard brass Yalies. Same with the doors from the tunnels to the basements."

"Which way do they open, chief?" the SEAL pursued.

Schultz stared off, biting his lower lip as he considered the question. "Pretty certain inward. Yeah. Towards you, if you're inside the tunnel," he confirmed. "That'll put the hinges on your side of the door," he added, knowing they'd have to be dismantled since the lock and hasp were on the opposite side. He waited but there were no other questions. "Oh. One other thing. Snakes. The whole damn base is overrun with snakes during the warm weather. Suspect they'll be a mess of them hibernating in those tunnels this time of year. Most are harmless black snakes but, you never know. Might be a few poisonous ones mixed in," he warned.

Cort made a note of it and thanked him for his assistance. "Okay. Let's go over the attack, now."

Chapter Eighteen

Leslie Pickens detested these confrontations with Lucerne, Gartland, Hemmings and Harrison; the four naysayers, as he had come to see them. He glanced at his watch, it was 10:30. Fifteen minutes to go and he'd be facing another wall of resistance. As if on cue, his chest muscles tensed and the throbbing in his head, now constant, grew more intense. It rankled him further that they had insisted Bennett not be included. Without his mentor he felt isolated and out gunned. Picking up his mug, he downed the remaining tepid coffee with one thirsty gulp. It was his fifth mug that morning and he instantly regretted it. The acidic response was yet another grim reminder that life had taken on a decidedly dismal aura since Thanksgiving and he cursed not the Iranians, but Lucerne and the others. Closing his eyes, he kneaded the ache in his stomach and tried resurrecting images of a less complicated life, specifically, the one he'd left behind as governor. But his reverie was short-lived.

Everyone arrived promptly and the meeting began as scheduled. Adding to his distress was the sea of somber expressions that gave no indication the problems confronting him had in any way diminished since their last bout together.

"Mr. President," Lucerne began immediately, "during the past twenty-four hours we have located the midshipmen and identified their captors."

Pickens couldn't believe his ears. Suddenly, he was awash with relief. With widened eyes and renewed enthusiasm, he said, "That's wonderful!" Then, leaning forward, he asked, "When do you expect to rescue them?" It hadn't registered that his exhilaration wasn't shared by the others.

"It's too soon to say."

Lucerne's cool response dampened his hope that soon all would be well again and he felt the euphoria slipping away.

"The SEALs have only just completed a preliminary recon and are now planning the assault phase of the operation," the Marine explained.

"You don't seem all that pleased, general. What's the problem?" he probed, not really wanting to hear it. "Do the terrorists know that we know?"

"We can't be certain but we're proceeding as though they do. There's good reason to believe part of their plan is to lure our men into a trap."

"Incredible! For what purpose?"

"There's ample evidence suggesting the terrorist leader is conducting a personal vendetta against our people, specifically, Admiral Harding and Commander Sampson. Consequently, we're moving cautiously."

"I should say. But, what does that mean in terms of rescuing the mids?" Pickens was already balancing the rescue against his low standing in the polls.

"It means," Lucerne continued, "the rescue is going to be touch and go. Not your standard counter-terrorist operation. We're dealing with a very sophisticated adversary, someone well versed in our tactics. We suspect he'll keep the mids alive for as long as he believes he's in control. If there's the slightest hint the balance is shifting away from him, he'll likely kill them."

Pickens slumped back into his chair. This wasn't such good news after all.

"Meanwhile," Lucerne went on, "he's using this kidnapping to elicit more than political ransom. For him, its a life and death game in which he gets to match wits against our SEALs. His goal seems to be to humiliate them by outsmarting and defeating them. By raising the stakes to that level," Lucerne said, "his chances of succeeding are tenuous and he knows it. The problem is that he's got a reputation for living on the edge, so there's no doubt he's calculated that into the equation."

"If this Commander Sampson's his target," Pickens asked, "why not replace him with someone else? That should defuse our man."

"Sampson's our best hope," Lucerne countered. "We can't remove him. He knows his antagonist better than anyone on the team. Besides, it's too late to consider it. With Sampson, we're putting the best we have against him," Lucerne said with a note of caution. "But, there are no guarantees. We'll need to proceed carefully and slowly. They can't just break in and rescue them. This will have to be an extremely well planned operation. If our assessment of this man is accurate, we must plan for all contingencies."

Shit, Pickens mused, another goddamn wrinkle. Every step forward brought with it another darker, more ominous specter making him wonder how much more complicated things could get. Sitting there under their stares, he felt his elation receding and in its place the start of a heavy depression.

Finally, envisaging his presidency teetering because of some crazed terrorist, he asked, "What's that translate to, general?"

"It'll require holding this information close while we assess their stronghold and formulate our attack."

Lucerne's terse response was clear - keep Bennett out of this and let us do our job. Once again, Pickens felt alienated from the men advising him. Pushing his chair away, he stood and began pacing in tight circles behind his desk. "What if we wait? Delay going in? Wouldn't that ameliorate the situation?" he muttered more to himself than to the others. "Or, we could deal with the Iranians after the mids are released. Hell, if we know where the mids are, why not just go in the day after the deadline? Wouldn't that confuse the terrorists? Let them think we capitulated and then, pow!" Spinning on his heel, he turned to his chief of staff, who, like the others, had been watching him in silent fascination. "What do you think, Daren?" asked the president.

The look that passed among the others wasn't missed by McCurdy. It was painfully obvious Pickens was unravelling.

"I, uh, don't know, Mr. President," he responded unsure of himself. "It seems a little late in the game to change the batting order."

That wasn't the response Pickens sought and he glared at the confused aide.

It was Hemmings' turn and, heaving a sigh, he said, "Mr. President, there are further complications to the Iranian invasion."

Pickens was perspiring now and massaging his stomach, unaware that he was doing so. His mind was transfixed on the notion of delaying the rescue. In his muddled brain it seemed like the best solution.

"What?" he said, as if noticing Hemmings for the first time. "What, now, Ray?" He withdrew his handkerchief and wiped the pasty saliva at the corners of his mouth.

"Iran has given the Royal Family an ultimatum," the CIA director informed him. "They either capitulate or Iran detonates tactical nuclear weapons in each of their two major cities, Riyadh and Jiddah."

Pickens' jaw dropped and his color drained. "Jesus Christ! That's insane! They can't do that!" he protested. Then, twisting his handkerchief, he asked, "Do they really have them or are they bluffing?"

"It's quite probable. A safe guess would be that they bought them from Russia," Hemmings said. "These are tactical nuclear weapons," he explained. "They're designed for battlefield employment rather than strategic ops. So, their collateral damage is minimal. With a comparatively low yield of less than ten kilotons, Mr. President, detonating them in an urban environment would wipe out, probably several square city blocks."

With that, the president's expression changed and he exclaimed with relief, "Oh. Well, that's not too bad. I thought you were talking another Hiroshima." Then, catching himself, he said to the stunned panel, "What I mean, is thank God they don't have strategic weapons." Speaking more cautiously, he asked, "How would they deliver them?"

"Transporting and setting them off is a relatively simple task," Hemmings informed him. "The damn things are only six to eight inches long, depending on what version they purchased, and can easily fit into a backpack. The radioactive contamination would be more of a factor than the destruction, rendering the explosion site useless for years. Imagine, if you will, the impact on our economy if we lost access to our major financial districts."

Pickens's eyes widened. "Shit! Whatever happened to nice little wars?" he said, as he turned to the window and the monuments beyond. Shaking his head, he muttered more to himself than to the others, "Everything gets so damn complicated." Then, looking into the distance, he mused loud enough for them to hear, "All we needed was a nice war. The public would've understood and supported that and we would've looked good again. Why couldn't they have just limited themselves to Iraq? We could have tolerated that. But, no. The greedy bastards had to go for the gold. Now we're facing nuclear weapons. God almighty! How easily things turn to shit around here. We can't have `em exploding nuclear weapons," he argued to himself. "No, sir. Not nukes. Even Russ would see the wisdom of preventing that." Pausing, he knitted his eyebrows while still rubbing the ache in his stomach. "Hmm, then again, maybe it doesn't matter." A smile broke across his face that the others couldn't see. "Maybe one war's as good as the next." He mulled that over a moment then dismissed the notion with a shrug. When he turned back to the others they were surprised to see he looked poised and less anxious. It was as if he'd transitioned to another plain. "Are there any alternatives, gentlemen?" he asked. "Or do we let them have Saudi Arabia? Obviously, we can't risk nuclear warfare." Then, before anyone could respond, he smiled and said, "For the sake of discussion, what difference does it make who we buy our oil from? Am I Right?"

The question and his detached, child-like expression suggested he had crossed the line. Without saying it, they knew he was now not only a danger to himself but to the country, as well.

Ignoring his foolish notion as if it hadn't been uttered, the defense secretary said in a gentle, fatherly tone, "Mr President, we have a few options that shouldn't be dismissed out of hand."

Pickens looked at the older man and, without breaking his smile, asked, "Really? What might they be?"

"Well," Gartland said, setting forth their already agreed upon agenda, "we feel it would be in our best interests to conduct a preemptive strike against Iran while going forward with the hostage rescue."

"You really think so?" the president asked without rancor.

"Yes.   We do, Mr. President," Gartland replied with a reassuring smile.

In the end, Pickens seemed content when they assured him, if one should fail, the other would not.

Chapter Nineteen

At Sampson's request, Harding declared a forty-eight hour security drill commencing at 0600. As a result, access to the naval station across the river was restricted to military personnel and civilian employees. Armed Marines took control of the gate from the civilian police force and no one could enter without a valid ID. Visitors and guests needing to conduct business on the base could come aboard only if accompanied by a military escort and only after being logged in. All vehicles entering, Navy and civilian, were stopped, pulled over and thoroughly searched. The command center and the grounds surrounding it were cordoned off from the rest of the base and declared off limits to personnel not issued a special security badge. Armed sentries patrolling the area on foot carried radios and stayed in close communication with the security force. Harding had personally made the announcement and emphasized the serious nature of the drill.

At 0730, Sampson met with the key players in the large, windowless briefing room. The room was filled. Those unable to sit, stood along the side and rear or sat in the aisle. Attendance was limited to his SEALs, selected FBI agents, army special forces helicopter crew chiefs, Maryland Highway Patrol officers, Secret Service agents, U. S. Park Police, officers from JCS and communications specialists from FEMA, NSA and Defense Communications. All held top secret clearances. Outside, a heavy, driving rain had been falling since before dawn.

Standing at the lectern, Sampson studied the somber faces, took a final sip of coffee and began. "Gentlemen," he said, in a slow cadence, "we're in the final phase of gathering hard intelligence. Two of our members infiltrated the target zone at approximately 0530 and have begun transmitting info to us via encrypted comms.

"We've learned the reason Dankworth hasn't posted sentries along the Bainbridge fence line is because he's wired the damn thing. The system he's using isn't very sophisticated but it will alert him if the field is broken. We've decided to leave it operational rather than take it out."

Noting a few puzzled faces, he explained, "Leaving it in place will give those monitoring it a false sense of security. And, since we won't be going through it, there's no reason to disable it. Anyway, by now Dankworth knows he's been targeted. Those helo flights throughout the night were a tip off. The FLIR readouts indicate that he's already tightened security, which is to our advantage." Again, he explained, "His limited crew can't remain on full alert indefinitely and be combat ready when we attack."

There was a general nodding of heads.

"Okay," he pressed on, "this is a quick and dirty rundown of the plan worked up by Cort and the Blue and Gold team leaders." He nodded toward the men in the front row. "After I've finished we'll split up with our respective support teams to work out the details. Unless our men inside give us a reason to change plans, we'll stay with this one.

"This is to be a two-pronged assault, coordinated down to the second. It will consist of a diversionary tactical force and a rescue-sniper force. The rescue team will enter the base two hours before the assault via the sewage outfall pipe right here...,"

As he spoke, a map was projected on the screen beside him and he pointed to the dotted line running south toward the river from the building marked *Sewage Disposal Plant*, located close to the fence line.

"...just below the old fire fighting school, here," he added, circling the spot on the map with his pointer for clarification.

"What if the pipe is impassible?" Cutler, the FBI agent, interrupted.

"It isn't, Floyd. That's how our guys went in. Last night, we severed the pipe seventy-five feet from the fence, across the road from the training center. We found it obstructed in a few places where tree roots entered through cracks. It's been cleared and it's now passable."

That seemed to satisfy the agent and he nodded while jotting something down in his note pad.

Sampson waited a moment. With no other questions, he continued. "Once inside the compound, the rescue and sniper teams will make their way to the old power house, where they'll enter the tunnel and follow it to where it divides. Alfa will go to this building, where the hostages are and Bravo will head for the one directly across from it."

He continued referring to the map as he spoke.

"Based on the blueprints and Chief Schultz's input, we know exactly where the tunnels emerge in each building. Once in place, Alfa and Bravo will wait until H-Hour. One hour before H-Hour, the Maryland Highway Patrol will close I-95 on both sides of the Susquehanna and re-route traffic east onto State 40 while burning up the airwaves with calls for assistance to handle a toxic chemical spill on southbound I-95, just north of the bridge. At the same time State Police move in and seal off Port Deposit. The sector will erupt with police and ambulance sirens, fire trucks and medivac helicopters all communicating distress messages."

A Secret Service agent in the rear asked, "How the hell are you going to get everyone to participate without blowing your cover? That's a lot of resources to pull in, commander."

"You're right. Other than the State Police and Highway Patrol, everything else will be done with smoke and mirrors. The fire trucks will come from Aberdeen, the medivac helos from U. S. Park Police, also flying out of Aberdeen. All radio comms will be scripted by FEMA and transmitted from a portable communications van to be located at Perry Point. To anyone monitoring those frequencies it should sound as if there's been a serious, life-threatening accident."

Cutler then said, "We're ready to hire you at the bureau whenever you're ready."

"One thing at a time," Sampson said. "Let's get through this one first. Now," he continued, "five minutes before H-Hour, two UH-60 Army Blackhawks loaded with SEALs will lift off and join the medivac helos that will be ferrying back and forth to the accident site from Aberdeen. At the river, they'll peel off, make a below-the-horizon approach to the target area and, at exactly 0130, pop up over this line of trees. One will hover above the quadrangle, here, between the two target buildings and the other does the same above the adjacent athletic field. We kick out the fast ropes and hit the ground while the tunnel doors are blown off. Alfa heads for the mids in building one while Bravo moves to the roof of building two. If all goes as planned, everyone'll be home for breakfast," he said with a smile. "Questions?"

For the next hour he and Cort provided specifics of the plan as they responded to questions, the first one from Harding.

"How're you going to coordinate Alfa and Bravo's role with the helo?" the admiral asked.

Cort stood and answered. "Encrypted comms, sir. Each man going in will carry a Motorola multi-channel radio with spare batteries. To keep the line of communications open with them, one man will remain in the power house as a relay and also to protect their rear."

Harding nodded, then asked, "What if your comms fail?"

"That's what I meant by well-coordinated, admiral," Sampson interjected. "We'll be working from a time line, starting from the moment we pre-position the Blackhawks, load our men and equipment aboard and launch. At precisely 0130, with or without comms, while we're sliding down those fast ropes, shooting at anything that moves, Alfa and Bravo teams are coming through the doors."

"What are the rules of engagement?" The question came from an army colonel with a JCS badge on his uniform.

Sampson recognized the special forces officer whom, he knew had been sent there as protection. Unless he objected, every aspect of the operation discussed in his presence had JCS's blessing. The question had been asked at Lucerne's insistence to get the response on the record. It was a subtle way of providing legal protection for the SEALs should anything go awry and some politician, in an attempt to save his own ass later, tried bringing them up for court martial. As long as JCS was in on the planning phase it could be assumed the president was briefed before the operation went down. Accusing the SEALs of malfeasance would drag in the Joint Chiefs and the president, something no politician, no matter how desperate, would do.

"They're quite simple," Sampson replied, matter-of-factly, "Shoot. Shoot. Look." It was the SEAL's standard way of conducting close-in fighting, where one relied on reflex combat skills honed by thousands of hours of training rather than waste a valuable second to determine if the first shot eliminated the enemy.

The colonel nodded. There was no mistaking the implications - no prisoners would be taken.

"What about command and control?" someone else asked.

"Admiral Harding is running the op," Sampson responded. "And I'm On Scene Commander. There'll be no comms with the admiral once we lift off until it's over or...," He hesitated and considered what he was about to say next while searching the faces of the younger, less experienced SEALs seated before him, "unless, we need backup."

"What form will the backup take?" probed the questioner.

"FBI SWAT teams providing perimeter security around the compound will be monitoring our comms. We'll call them in if they're needed."

"They're en route to Aberdeen now," Cutler said, loud enough for everyone to hear without turning to face the man who asked. "They'll be at your disposal," he said confidently to Sampson, who responded with a raised thumb.

When asked about weapons, Sampson responded, "We'll be loaded. Dankworth has never been known to skimp in that area. The Blackhawks will each have 7.62 mini guns and 50 caliber machine guns with 2000 rounds of linked clips. Alfa will carry room-clearing weapons that include flash bangs, carbine-15 rifles and 92 SBF Beretta pistols, making them light and fast. Bravo, which will control the quad and athletic fields from atop building two, will be loaded out with light machine guns with 800 rounds each and 50 caliber sniper rifles with 30 rounds each. Blue and Gold will have assorted weapons including M-16s and Berettas.

Those in the second helo will have everything they need to clear their target buildings and to provide ground cover from those buildings."

"It's going to look like the invasion of Normandy, Tom," Harding said. "You can't extract the mids under that fire."

"No, sir. We won't. We'll take them out through the tunnel. If, for any reason we can't do that, we'll hold them secure in the basement until it's over."

It was nearly noon when they had finished. The air was charged as the combat veterans, like horses at the gate, ached to enter the fray. Their enthusiasm, as Sampson knew, was infectious and the younger SEALs along with the support personnel were also feeling a buzz of anticipation. Sampson remained behind with Harding and the others while Cort and his men left for Aberdeen to begin test firing their weapons and assembling their gear. It would be close to dusk before Sampson would rendezvous with them again. In the interim, intel from within the compound revealed Dankworth had outfitted his men with Russian AK-47 assault rifles and RPD light machine guns. His army, it was reported, seemed to be evenly divided between Americans and Cubans. According to one transmission, they were *mean looking mothers*, who carried and handled their weapons like combat veterans.

* * *

"Trish, how you holding up?" The caller's seemingly genuine concern for her well-being disarmed her and she responded with much less anger than previous times.

"I'm okay," she said, wearily. Like the others, she too was feeling the pressure.

She glanced around the newsroom and noted with satisfaction that no one seemed to be looking in her direction. Having succeeded until now in keeping this intrigue and her role in it a secret, she was anxious to keep it that way. Uncertain of her motivations, she suspected it was the very real prospect of a Pulitzer Prize-winning series or, at the very least, a lucrative book deal. In preparing the story, she had read about the Stockholm syndrome, in which hostages come full circle and identify with their captors, much as Patricia Hearst had claimed after being abducted by the Symbionese Liberation Army in the early seventies. Listening now to Dankworth's mellow, non-threatening voice, she wondered if she, too, could be experiencing something similar. Perhaps, she conjectured, it was a combination of the two. Of one thing she was certain. Like the rest of the players in this drama, from Pickens on down, she was physically and mentally drained.

She'd been on a tightrope since the first phone call. And the fitful nights of sleep since finding the dead midshipman had only weakened her resolve further. Beneath her outward bravado her nerves were raw. On top of that, she was convinced she was being spied upon and followed. Entering her car and apartment, acts she'd performed routinely, now gave her pause and required courage and fortitude. She could do neither without first peering nervously into every shadowy corner, not knowing what or who might be waiting for her. Meanwhile, loud, unanticipated noises and late night phone calls left her frightened and trembling. In the dark she saw images of dead and beaten mids. Of course, what she didn't know, was that she was responding as Dankworth had intended.

"Good. I was worried about you. You've been through a hell of an ordeal," he said. She found his words and tone soothing. "It's almost over, Trish. You won't have to tolerate much more."

"That's a relief," she replied, forgetting for the moment that the mids, and not she, were the victims. "What's next on your agenda?"

"Oddly," he confessed, "it has to do with you. I have a proposition which I'm offering as compensation for all your troubles."

"Proposition? Sounds like there are strings attached. What makes you think I'd agree to anything you have to offer?" The question was posed without malice.

"Because it's a payback for what I've put you through. It's my way of closing the books while doing myself a small favor. That is, if my instincts are correct."

"Boy, you sure know how to charm a girl," she said with a chuckle. "After all this, you want me to do you a favor? That takes brass balls."

Dankworth returned the laugh. "I'm glad you haven't lost your sense of humor, Trish. Please, just hear what I have to say before deciding. Okay?"

Intrigued, she agreed.

"I've been telling you from the beginning this is the story of the century. And you're the only one who can write it. The only problem is that you'll be writing it from one perspective - the government's. I want to offer you an opportunity to see it from mine, too, Trish. I figure they're pretty close to coming in and rescuing the mids and in a short time I'll be dead. Wouldn't it be a real scoop if you got my side of the story before they get me? You know, a personal profile. How the Iranians recruited me. My role in this operation. How we did what we did and why we selected these mids? If you don't get it from me, Trish, you aren't going to get it because the best Sampson and those guys can come up with will be speculation." He paused, allowing her to consider it.

"What makes you so sure, you're not coming out of this thing alive?" she asked, skeptically.

"Trish," he said with a conspirator's voice, "I'm not going to survive because that's the way I want it. If I got away, where would I go? I can't remain in the U. S. and I sure as hell ain't gonna live in Iran. Besides, the Iranians will want me dead, anyway. When the smoke clears those rug heads won't want me around. I can link them to the kidnapping, which they've been denying all along. Invading a neighboring country happens all the time. It's global politics. But, kidnapping, murder, terrorism, that's something different. The international community doesn't tolerate it and somebody's got to be held accountable. Look at those buffoons in Libya. They've still got to answer for downing that PanAm plane over Scotland. Naw," he paused, reflectively, "without me around, they're off the hook."

Had she detected a hint of melancholy in his voice? Thoughts of the Pulitzer clouded her mind and she found his logic flawless. She had vowed from the beginning not to allow any opportunity to slip through her fingers. With Harding's help, and Mrs. Bennett's, too, she had documented every aspect of this story. Every aspect but one. And now she had a chance to nail that one down, too.

"What is it that you want me to do?" she asked.

"Simple. Meet me. We'll talk and after hearing my side, if you wish, I'll take you to the mids. You can bring a camera but," his voice suddenly turned hard, "you cannot alert anyone, especially Sampson. This is just between the two of us. Sampson will get his turn at me later."

The idea was tempting and intriguing. In her mind, she was already writing that aspect of the story. Discarding any concern for her safety, she leapt at the opportunity and agreed to meet him at seven that evening in southeast Baltimore.

Following his directions, she found herself in the center of a blighted industrial site, just off the I-95 O'Donnell Street ramp, on the north side of the Baltimore Tunnel. Anticipating the rush hour, made worse by the heavy rain, she had allowed herself two hours and was pleased when she arrived twenty minutes early. As a precaution, she drove around the stark neighborhood, surveying the area, before parking where he'd told her, next to a vacant lot encased in a high chainlink fence. Hers was the only car on either side of the dark street, made darker by the broken street lights and the shadows of adjoining buildings. She shut off the engine and waited in the stillness, listening and peering out at the night. The only sound came from the pounding rain on the roof. It was steady and unrelenting. Soon, the car cooled and the dampness settled in. With the doors locked and the windows tightly closed, it didn't take long before the glass began misting up, further isolating her from the harsh surroundings.

When seven o'clock arrived and passed she feared another plot to draw her away from her apartment. Finally, at seven-ten, through the distorted rush of water down the windshield and the dewy circles she'd wiped with her glove, she saw the outline of someone approaching. Tense and nervous, she reached up and cleared the glass again and strained to see him more clearly. She thought of turning on the headlights but changed her mind as he neared. It took a while but once she made him out she realized he couldn't be the terrorist. He was old and frail and walked with a partial limp and she dismissed him as a lost soul trudging through the night. When he paused a few yards in front of her and hunched over and peered inside, she pressed her locks down again and held her breath. She couldn't make out his face and she hoped he couldn't see hers, either. After a long, tense moment in which she remained perfectly still, he straightened and proceeded slowly past her. She tried following his image in the rear view mirror but he quickly merged with the darkness. Once again, she was alone in the steamed up car, unable to distinguish much beyond the outer edges of her car. Concluding that he might be delayed because of the rain, she decided to give him ten more minutes. If he didn't show by then, she'd leave. After giving the windshield a final swipe, she wrapped her coat tight around her and focused her attention down the street to the vague outline of the city's lights in the distance. For an instant, she thought she noted movement in the street to her left. That was just before her window smashed and she felt a powerful force against her jaw.

* * *

Whenever rain continued at the rate it had been falling, it was standard procedure for the attendant at the Conowingo Dam, five miles up river from Port Deposit, to monitor the water level while maintaining a steady dialogue with the National Weather Service. He needed to know how long the front bringing the rain would linger over the region. He also received periodic reports from the Pennsylvania Department of Interior advising him of the amount of rainfall measured along the rambling Susquehanna River and its tributaries. Using an uncomplicated math table he could then easily calculate how much water he needed to release to relieve the building pressure against the dam. Shortly afterwards, he'd lower the spillway and tons of water would surge toward the broad Chesapeake, raising the river three to four feet in minutes. It was a process he'd followed routinely for over twelve years. Weather permitting, and as an added safety precaution, he usually scheduled it during the early morning hours, when there was no boat traffic down river. In an emergency, he could always release the water during the day, but that would require setting off a series of high pitched sirens mounted on poles along the river's edge to alert boaters and barge operators to secure their craft.

On this night, based upon the data, he concluded the task needed to be done within the next twelve hours and he made a decision that around 1:30 that morning would be best.

Chapter Twenty

The late afternoon meeting of the NSC executive members, convened by Vice President Louis Mack was intended to be brief and focused. Of necessity, it would address only Pickens' state of mind and an appropriate response to the Iranian crisis. Until that moment rumors had been circulating within the tight knit group about his well-being but, except for those who had actually witnessed the president's meltdown, there was only speculation.

Mack, who was twenty years senior to the president, looked somber and concerned as he addressed the group. "Gentlemen," he said, "there's been an unexpected turn of events requiring our full attention and unanimity. It saddens me to report that our president has suffered a minor setback."

At his insistence, the session was off the record. But still, he chose his words carefully, not wishing to undermine the man during a time of personal crisis. As an elder statesman within his party, he had never been a fan of Pickens, whom he considered a shallow, unrefined politico. His decision to balance the ticket had been a painful one, made reluctantly, after a series of consultations with his party's leaders. Now, putting his personal feelings aside to solidify those around him, he said, "Shortly after lunch today, President Pickens confined himself to bed complaining of severe stomach pain and accompanying headaches. As you know, he's been under considerable stress and his refusal to leave his quarters today to deal with the Iran issue must be viewed with extreme concern." There was no enmity in his tone as he spoke, only an urgency for the matter at hand.

As he expected, the disclosure was greeted with introspective silence in a room where the mood was as dismal as the raw weather outside.

"Under the circumstances," he went on, "I insisted that he be examined by the White House physician, and the president agreed. The initial assessment is that the president is suffering from acute anxiety which, as you can surmise, began several days ago and has now disabled him. At my urging the Chief of Psychiatry at

Bethesda has been consulted and he, too, agrees with the diagnosis. On a positive note, with rest and proper medication, the president should be back to battery shortly."

"What does `shortly' translate to?" Diamond wanted to know.

"Given that he has withdrawn himself from the source of the stress," Mack replied, without attempting to disguise the problem, "that should be several days after the matter with Iran has been resolved."

"In the meantime...?" Diamond pressed.

"In the meantime," the vice president said, "with the president's full concurrence I am declaring him out of the loop on the Iranian issue."

As he had expected, there was no opposition. Pickens had left them rudderless in a major storm. In contrast, they were all familiar with Mack's position, which, like an anchor to windward, had remained constant. From the onset he had fully backed Lucerne and Hemmings and, on several occasions had even attempted to persuade Pickens to follow their advice, only to be put off by his promise to weigh all sides. Which was Pickens' way of telling his vice president to *stay out of it.*

Now, envisioning problems, Hemmings said, "Before addressing the gulf issue, Mr. Vice President, I believe it would be prudent to establish a cover story for the president's illness. Something that won't give the Iranians or our allies, for that matter, cause to question our resolve if his predicament should leak out."

Mack nodded. "I've already anticipated that contingency. Fortunately, time and circumstances are on our side. He has no scheduled public appearances between now and the deadline imposed by Iran, two days hence. We will, therefore, carry on White House business as usual. Daren, here, will advise the staff that Pickens is working out of his quarters in an effort to ward off the early signs of the flu and that he should be back to battery by Monday morning. Meanwhile, the doctors have prescribed a sedative, which will allow him to rest comfortably while we work this problem. Unless he has a major turn for the worse, I'm confident we'll get through these next forty-eight hours without drawing attention to his dilemma."

That seemed to satisfy everyone.

"Now," Mack continued in a manner that left no doubt of his resolve, "if fortune holds, in ten hours the midshipmen will be rescued. That operation is well underway and there isn't anymore any of us can do except to pray." He glanced at Lucerne as he spoke. He knew the general well and had suffered in silence with him throughout his ordeal. "It's critical that we now shift our focus to the gulf and make preparations to take the appropriate actions at the appropriate time." Addressing Lucerne, he asked, "What are our military options, John?"

"We have several," the general replied. He then reviewed each of them for the vice president, who had not been kept up to speed by Pickens.

When he concluded, Hemmings suggested a timetable beginning with issuing a demarche to Iran's UN ambassador condemning their acts of military aggression. "It must be issued," he asserted, "with the full concurrence of the Security Council, the Arab states and the major industrialized nations."

"I agree," Mack said. Then, turning to the Deputy Secretary of State, he asked, "How quickly can we move on this?"

"Immediately," Harrison replied.

Lucerne had a problem with that and he said, "I recognize that the fuse is short but, if we can delay contacting the other nations a bit longer, I prefer waiting until the rescue goes down. We're only hours away. And since we don't know the extent to which the Iranians are controlling the terrorists, I believe it would be wise not to tip them off."

"Point taken," Mack said. "Can State work around that?" he asked Harrison.

"We can and we will," he said. "We'll commence notifying the others as soon as you give us the go-ahead, general."

Mack noted that for the first time since the kidnapping the NSC was functioning unanimously and harmoniously. The way it should have been from day one. Then, unleashing some pent up anger, he said to Harrison, "This charade has gone far enough. It's time to back up words with deeds. I want those bastards to know we mean business. When you do deliver that demarche, I want it to be accompanied by an ultimatum. We're not simply going to condemn their acts of aggression. I intend to prevent them. Please prepare for my review a paper telling the Iranians to stand down their air forces and to recall all naval and amphibious forces back to port immediately, including the two Kilos in the northern Arabian Sea." His face reddened as he continued. "And, general, I want a list of primary and secondary targets for my approval. And also put the Annapolis and the carrier task force on ready alert."

The discussion continued at a heated pace as they moved to make up for lost time, with Mack detailing a series of communiques he wanted sent to allies alerting them of his intentions. And, while the tone would be to garner their support, the clear message was that we would proceed without it if necessary. When they finally concluded, the vice president promised to join Lucerne, Hemmings and Diamond at the Pentagon's Military Command Center later to await word of the rescue.

*   *   *

The gray daylight yielded swiftly to winter darkness while the rain continued unabated. Sampson, his adrenalin pumping, peered through the partially opened hangar doors at the perimeter road. In the distance, Aberdeen's workers were filing off the base unaware of the military force being staged just a half mile away in the sealed hangar at Phillips Air Field. Though his gaze was fixed upon the distant ribbon of taillights inching toward the main gate his mind was steadfastly working out each detail of the assault. Like a computer, he segregated each aspect of the operation, analyzed it and then fitted it into the larger matrix. At every step in the process, as he had done repeatedly that day, he tried anticipating what might go wrong and how it might go wrong. He had just checked the weather report for the third time and confirmed again that the front which had brought the rain, would remain firmly rooted over the mid-Atlantic region throughout the night. He looked up at the laden sky and smiled. SEALs loved water in any form.

Scooping out the depleted plug of tobacco wedged behind his lower lip, he tossed it onto the puddled tarmac and watched it dissipate under the pelting rain. Then, turning, he surveyed the scene behind him again. The buzz of activity, accented by the resonating sounds of gear being moved about and the high pitched crackle of radio comms within the vaulted hangar might give the untrained observer the impression the complex mission had fallen behind schedule. But he knew better. A veteran of hundreds of special operations, he took comfort in watching his team of well-honed professionals prepare for combat.

Spaced evenly apart were three Blackhawks, two for the mission and a backup. Each was separated by its own start-up generator and stacks of weapons and ammunition. The efficiency of the two military services meshing reminded Sampson of a well-choreographed ballet. In a final inspection of engines and rotors, the helo crews were crawling over and through the powerful machines that would take Sampson and his men to battle, while their crewmates attended to the gunships' armaments. Working alongside them, Red Cell's Blue and Gold teams were busy securing braided, nylon fast ropes to the telescopic bars mounted into the helos' overhead for the 120-foot drop into the quadrangle later that night. Their lives and those of their teammates would depend on how well they did their job. Next, the SEALs would begin loading their gear and the weapons they had test fired earlier.

Off to the side, clusters of men in black jump suits, their faces blackened, spoke quietly among themselves as they sorted and prepared their special implements of warfare. There were wire cutters, radio packs, flares, K-Bar knives to be stuffed into boots, face masks, night scopes, small, powerful drills - in sum, everything needed to remove obstacles and destroy an enemy. Everyone had a task and they worked to the steady beat of the rain that hammered the corrugated roof with the menace of a thousand drums.

179

The hours passed and soon every piece of gear was stowed in the Blackhawks and for a while there was an eerie stillness. To maintain the fighters' night vision the bright overhead lights were shut off. Only the soft glow of red lights illuminated the hangar now, as men sat around in quiet reflection hugging their weapons. Occasionally, an undecipherable chirp would come from Harding's portable command post parked in the rear of the hangar and the men would strain to listen, knowing Sampson and Cort were in there with the admiral going over the op one final time.

At 10:15 Sampson came out of the trailer and wandered over to the maroon civilian van. He smiled as he read the mustard-yellow logo painted on it earlier.

> Pete's Plumbing Service, Inc.
> Heating, Air Conditioning & Electrical
> Havre de Grace, MD
> For 24 Hour Service - Call 410-555-1605

"How you doin', Timmy?" he asked the tallest of the five men gathered around the vehicle.

In addition to their fighting and underwater skills, every SEAL had acquired a sub-specialty. Some were medical corpsmen, others pilots or radio techs and others, like Fester, were rock climbers. When melded into a unit, they possessed all the talent needed to overtake and destroy any fortress. Timmy's expertise was explosives. He could dismantle any bomb, most of them blindfolded. And likewise, he could construct the most lethal device using ordinary household products, if necessary. Sampson and Timmy were about the same age and, in the small community of SEALs, their careers had intertwined over the years. They'd served together on supersecret missions, most recently in the Middle East and Bosnia. Unlike Sampson, who was of average height but muscular, Timmy was built like a bear, large and powerful. Nearly as broad as he was tall, he had the strength of four men. Yet, his soft southern drawl, easy-going personality and disarming belly laugh conveyed the image of a gentle giant. It was an image he nurtured but one that also made him the target of unprovoked barroom brawls in which invariably he was the only one left standing. And, while he also appeared slow and ungainly that, too, was misleading. During an op he could move with the stealth and cunning of a fox and be counted on to analyze events with uncanny precision. For this mission, Sampson had designated him leader of Alfa and Bravo teams.

"Doin' good," he replied with his trademark baritone laugh. "Ready for bear."

"Good," Sampson said as he gathered Timmy's men around for one final rundown.

Like their shipmates, they were all combat tested and eager to begin the task of following the florescent paint trail left for them by the two men already inside the compound. When illuminated with a black light, the markings would provide two important bits of information; the safest route to the power plant and the last time Dankworth's men had crossed it. The last transmission from inside was at 9:50, when the infiltrators had indicated the sewage pipe was still open and unguarded. Had it not been, Timmy and his men would have had to enter the compound by crawling through the less-protected, shallow trench dug earlier as a contingency beneath the fence near the reservoir and beside the state road.

Tucked inside their rubber-lined pockets, each man in Timmy's squad carried a laminated photo of the base and a schematic of the interior of the buildings they would occupy. They were the same aids issued to everyone in the op, including the helo crews and the FBI agents. Each was overlaid with a simple grid of numbers and letters, a technique enabling anyone inside to rapidly communicate his position or the enemy's if he needed to call in fire support. It was one more precaution Sampson was taking. Certain that Dankworth would be monitoring all open frequencies, as well as the encrypted ones he couldn't decode, Sampson used this system to minimize transmissions, even the coded ones, since increased radio comms could be a signal of imminent action.

At 10:45 the hangar doors parted wide enough for the van to drive through. As it passed him, Sampson slapped the side panel, a final signal to Timmy and the other four men concealed in the rear that he wished them well. He stood there leaning against the heavy door, ignoring the spray of cold rain against his face while watching the taillights until they finally disappeared. As in every other op, he was suppressing a knot of anxiety that gnawed like a cancer at his gut. Though they rarely spoke of it they all shared it in the early stages of every op. But they also knew how to master it so that it would be gone and forgotten when they entered the target area. He checked his watch. In fifteen minutes Timmy and the others would be dropped off on the county road and from there make their way to the sewer pipe. If all went well, Sampson would next see them herding a group of frightened and dazed midshipmen into the welcoming arms of their rescuers.

Meanwhile, in the basement of building one, Ingrid tried making sense of the sudden stepped-up activity among the guards. The increased and hurried foot traffic above her was unusual for that late hour. She also noticed with concern, those bringing in the evening meal were not wearing their usual khaki outfits but had changed into dark clothes. And, for the first time, they carried side arms. They were also tense and anxious. Even the one who had begun joking with the mids, was now distracted and decidedly hostile.

A short while later the movement subsided dramatically and, as her classmates settled in for the night, she strained to listen for other signs of change. Then, at 11:00, the door burst open and a guard entered. He walked menacingly to Ingrid, ignoring the others. She knew him only from a distance and had an instinctive fear of him. He was ruggedly handsome and sinewy and wore his long, blonde hair pulled tightly into a pony tail. From the deference paid him by the other guards, she had concluded he was one of the leaders, perhaps even Dankworth's second in command. Twice she had caught him leering at her; first, when they arrived and, again later, when he looked in and found her using the bucket. Several times thereafter, he either glanced in when the guards were delivering their food or came randomly on his own, each time lingering back in the doorway but saying nothing. Until now, he hadn't entered, which had eased her anxiety a bit.

Now, he stood over her but again, he remained mute. She in turn, refused to meet his gaze. Like a silent duel, each of them held their ground under the fearful stares of the others until he leaned down and released her from her bonds. He grabbed her arm and she resisted. She pulled away but he was strong and he held her and yanked her to her feet. Now, when she looked at him, he was grinning. It was the first time she'd been unshackled and, though cold and sore from the dampness that had settled into the ground from the rain, she didn't wish to be released by him. Again, she resisted but her efforts only caused him to tighten his vise-like grip.

Suddenly and unexpectedly, Bennett began shouting, "Let go of her! Do you hear me?" he insisted. "I said, let her go!"

The terrorist's dropped his smile and that gave Bennett ample warning to shield himself when he kicked at him. Distracted by Ingrid's resistance, his heavy boot missed Bennett's ribs and grazed off his shoulder instead, clipping the mid in the ear and sending him back against the wall. When she saw him readying another kick, Ingrid broke free and ran for the door. Forgetting Bennett, the guard quickly grabbed her before she went too far. And, twisting her arm, he shoved her into the hall and slammed the door shut.

Her sudden and unexpected removal from their midst left the mids nervous and unsettled, including the girl who had been raped and who had begun responding to her classmates' pleas. Now, with their leader gone, she and the others felt their resolve dissipating.

Meanwhile, Ingrid felt a swell of pride as she heard Bennett shouting for her return. But his voice soon faded as her captor pushed her before him down the long hall. At one point he paused before Dankworth's partially opened door and allowed her a glimpse inside. The scene frightened her and she gasped. She hadn't known of any other prisoners and she shuddered at seeing the partially nude, young woman lying across Dankworth's bunk. The left side of her face was bloodied and bruised and she seemed dazed. Her skirt was pushed up over her stomach and she had one hand manacled to a nearby pipe. The other one lay protectively over her exposed parts. Her blouse was open, revealing red slashes across her breasts, like the ones Ingrid had seen on her classmate. Beside the woman, hanging from a broken chair like a trophy, were her torn bikini panties and her bra. Hearing Ingrid's gasp, she turned her head and looked imploringly through bruised eyes. Unable to speak because of the tape across her mouth, she pulled vainly at her shackle.

When Ingrid moved towards the woman, her captor yanked her back to him. The contempt in her eyes when she turned and faced him was met with a cruel, hateful laugh. He shoved her forward again and she heard Dankworth call out, "Enjoy her, Sonny. But be careful," he said, laughing, "her daddy's a bad ass mareeeen." Then she heard him taunt his captive. "Ready for more, Trish?"

They proceeded a bit farther down the hall before the one called, Sonny, pushed her into a room and slammed the door behind him. The bare tiled room had been stripped of most of its fixtures but their was no mistaking its use. It reeked of urine and feces. Several cracked toilets lined one wall and fittings hung loosely where sinks and shower stalls had once been.

Immediately, she made a fist with her uninjured hand while backing away. She searched for something with which to defend herself but there was nothing, not a pipe or shard of glass. Nor was there anything to put between them. The room was long and narrow with no place to hide. Without electricity, the only light came from a low volt, battery-powered lantern, affixed high above the door.

"Strip, sweetheart," he said as he walked to her. He spoke with a thick German accent.

"No, way" she shouted defiantly while backing into a corner. "You can go to hell first, you Nazi bastard. Come near me and I'll cripple you for life."

His impassive expression never changed as he walked over and punched her in the stomach. She crumbled, gasping at his feet. As she struggled to breathe he reached down, grabbed a knot of hair and pulled her face to his crotch. "Now, *liebchen*, you please me with your mouth or I blow your fucking head off.

Verstanden?" His voice was hard and venomous and it seemed he would derive as much pleasure from either act.

He held her down by twisting her hair tighter and pressing her against the wall with his knee. And when she attempted to pull away he pushed his gun beneath her eye, digging the cold metal deeper when she resisted. She saw his finger against the trigger and she prayed the safety wasn't off.

"Come, come, darling. I haven't all night. We must have sex before the game. Now, do what I order or I shall kill you."

The deed took only a few minutes and he didn't care that she gagged and spit it out when he'd finished. In fact, that seemed to please him. It was a cold, brutal act intended more to demean her than satisfy him. Backing away, he zipped himself like an automaton then pulled her up and led her back down the hall to her room. Oddly, he didn't bind her. Instead, he shoved her inside as though discarding a bag of trash and locked the door. It was the first time she was able to move about and the unexpected freedom quickly dispelled the revulsion she had felt minutes before.

She leaned against the heavy door and listened while her classmates looked on in silence. Straining to hear if someone was on the other side, she could think only of the woman she'd seen earlier and of trying to escape. Hearing no one, she tried the door but it had been securely bolted. Then, turning to her friends, she darted among them trying vainly to undo their bonds while whispering reassurances to each of them.

Several hundred feet away, Timmy and the others snapped the lock on the powerhouse and entered the small, dank building. He checked the time. It was 12:05. It had taken fifteen minutes to reach the sewer pipe after exiting the van and another fifteen before all were safely inside the fence line. Moving cautiously in teams of two with ten yards between them, and Timmy in the rear, they had followed the fluorescent markings to within a hundred yards of the powerhouse before having to stop. As Alfa was about to leave the cover of the trees they spotted two of Dankworth's sentries keeping dry beneath the overhang of one of the few remaining Navy buildings. Unfortunately for the SEALs, the structure sat on a small rise above the Tome school grounds, giving them an unobstructed view of the open field that lay between the SEALs and their objective.

"What's the fucking problem?" Timmy whispered, when he reached the spot and found the others waiting there. They had spread themselves out in a semi-circle at the tree line, lying face down in the cold mud behind a nest of bare shrubs approximately fifteen yards from their quarry.

His question was answered with a nod and a motion suggesting they take the guards out.

"Negative," he replied after a moment. "Too risky. Might tip the others. We'll hafta go around," he whispered, pointing to the area away from the school that would take them in a wide arc behind the building and, in the process, slow their progress. "Alfa," he directed, "go first, we'll cover. When you're on the other side, give two squirts."

The signal would be sent by rapidly depressing the radio's transmit button twice without speaking, which, in turn, would be acknowledged with one squirt as Bravo prepared to follow. The sequence would be repeated again before Timmy started out.

The detour had cost them ten minutes but the delay wasn't crucial. They had allowed two hours to get into position and there was still plenty of time to traverse the tunnels. Before entering the powerhouse Timmy shone his black light on the wall next to the door and found the grid letter and number denoting where the two SEALs who had infiltrated the compound nearly twenty hours earlier had positioned themselves for the fire fight, info they had already passed via secure radio to Sampson back at Aberdeen.

At 12:15, Timmy took up his rear guard position in the power house while Alfa and Bravo climbed down into the tunnels.

They hadn't gone twenty feet when the lead SEAL bellowed, "Oh, fuck!"

"What?" whispered another, behind him.

"Snakes. Fucking place is loaded with them," came the response while his flashlight beam danced among tangled pockets of Black and King snakes.

The others found his distress amusing. "What're you worried about?" one SEAL teased. "You've eaten enough of them so's

186

they probably think you're one of `em. Besides, the mothers are hibernating. Look," he said, poking a nest with his rifle, "they're catatonic. Anyway, they're not poisonous," he continued with bravado as he reached down and retrieved a knot of snakes and held them inches from his face. "Hi ya, ya little fuckers," he said, before kissing the head of one.

The others watched the lethargic snakes as they stared back with glassy eyes.

"Come on, put `em down and let's move," the marksman from Bravo said to his partner.

"Okay. But first,...," the one holding them said. And, with the speed of a jungle predator he bit off one snake's head. Grinning, he held it between his teeth until the others had shown their approval. Then spitting it out, he said as he tossed the pack to the stone floor, "There, don't mess with a Navy SEAL!"

The others shook their heads. "You're fucking crazy," one said. "Like to see you do that with a rattler."

"Shit," his partner said, "I've seen him bite a rat's head off. Rattler's don't scare him."

Ten minutes later the teams had split up and were at their posts dismantling the door hinges, the incident with the snake a distant memory.

D Minus One

Chapter Twenty-One

At the sound of distant sirens and helos, Dankworth came running down the hall to the man monitoring the police scanner.

"What's happening?" he shouted, his adrenalin surging.

The radioman gave Dankworth a curious look. "Just an accident on I-95. Sounds pretty bad. Some kinda toxic shit. They closed a section of the highway, started re-routing traffic and gettin' folks to leave their homes." The incident didn't seem to alarm him as it did Dankworth.

"How long's this been going on?" Dankworth's mind was racing as he heard the emergency transmissions and requests for assistance.

"Accident report came over 'bout twenty-five minutes ago. They're just startin' to respond. Why? You got a problem, Bull?"

"Maybe. Could be a cover," he said, stroking his chin. He picked up the portable radio beside the scanner and said, "Bull to lookout one."

"Lookout one," the man in the clock tower responded immediately.

"What do you see?"

"Looks like helos along the interstate, Bull."

"Anything else?"

"Yeah. Coupla state police cars just headed down to the town. What's up?"

"Don't know yet. Everyone in place up there?" Dankworth had deployed his forces earlier, instructing them to prepare for anything.

"Armed and ready."

"Good. Stay alert." Next he called the other posts. "You heard what I told the tower. This could be nothing or the real thing," he warned everyone on the net. "Keep your eyes open and shoot anything that moves."

The men he'd selected were all combat tested mercenaries and in some cases had seen more action than the younger men on Sampson's team. And like their adversaries, they were eager to meet their foes.

There was an intensity in Dankworth's expression when he swept back into the room that made Trish instinctively press against the wall in a feeble attempt to distance herself from him, but it wasn't necessary. Ignoring her, he moved to the metal footlocker in the far corner and unsnapped the brass lock. He was like an animal in the wild, she thought, keeping his head cocked against the piercing sounds from outside the compound while preparing himself for battle. Believing this to be the prelude to his showdown with Sampson, she watched and prayed that whatever was about to happen would take him away and that he'd not return. He moved swiftly and systematically. Retrieving his K-Bar knife, he stuffed the long blade inside his boot then strapped on a set of shoulder holsters and filled them with a pair of matching 9mm Glocks. Next, he fastened a small radio to his web belt along with extra ammo clips. In minutes, he was a walking arsenal. Then, grabbing an assault rifle and several clips, he stepped into the hall and shouted, "Sonny." An instant later Trish heard him alert the German to get ready. This time, when he returned he unshackled her.

"Please," she begged him through her gag but he seemed not to hear.

Grasping her arm, he led her through the hall to the first floor, where she glimpsed other armed men in dark wool watch caps and blackened faces positioned behind barricaded windows. In the next moment, she was in the quadrangle with the cold rain lashing at her wounds. When she flinched he tightened his grip. Then, pulling her along like a piece of baggage, they trotted down the potholed road toward the gray outline of a building in the distance. Running into the rain with her mouth tapped made breathing difficult but she managed to suck in enough air to keep up with him. Her discomfit, though, was eclipsed by her fear that this was the finale to the drama she'd been living the past week. Twice she stumbled but he held her and propelled her forward with his strength. Upon reaching the building he charged the door with his shoulder, forcing it off its hinges with a harsh cracking sound. In the next instant, cold and drenched, she was standing in a pitch dark room with no clue of its parameters. Unlike her captor, who had memorized the floor plan and could move in the blackness with feline confidence, she remained paralyzed while he decided her fate. A moment later he was shoving her forward while she instinctively resisted. But he prevailed and soon he was forcing her into a corner at the far end of the large room.

He pressed her down into a crouching position and whispered, "Move and your dead." A moment later he was gone.

Bewildered but alert, she flattened herself against the wall and tried making sense of the distant sirens and the steady drone of helicopters while tracing Dankworth's hastened footsteps as he moved sequentially from one distant room to another. For a brief moment she thought of running for the door but reconsidered when she heard him nearby. Instead, she peeled off her gag. And though painful, she welcomed the chance to fill her lungs with the cold, night air. Meanwhile, Dankworth had stopped moving and she thought perhaps he'd left her there alone but then she heard his heavy breathing not twenty feet away.

"Sonny," she heard him call into his radio. "Bull, here. Do it now," he directed. "Do you read me?"

"Roger. Roger," came the crackling response, then silence.

At Dankworth's command the German appeared in the doorway before the uncomprehending mids grasping a bulging knapsack in his left hand. He stepped inside and with a sickening grin, announced, "It is party time, *kinder*." Then, he hooked the bag onto a nail behind the door. Lifting the flap, he reached inside and withdrew a length of wire which he unraveled and ran down under the door. When he'd finished, he paused, looked around and said, "Pleasant dreams and *Auf Wiedersehen*."

Still unaware, they watched with morbid fascination as he exited and bolted the door behind him. Then, with renewed terror, they understood what he'd done as the arming wire went taut and was pulled from the bag and out beneath the door.

Meanwhile, up river, Jack Sweetman sat at his small console in the control tower above the dam and dialed the phone number he'd memorized years earlier. As he waited, he hummed a mindless tune while looking down at the massive flood gates below and gauging the amount of water that would soon be flowing over them. He waited patiently as the phone rang at the Pennsylvania Electric Company headquarters in Philadelphia, sixty-seven miles away. He was accustomed to the delay. It was never picked up right away at this time of the morning. Cradling the phone between his head and shoulder, Sweetman reached for his thermos, unscrewed the lid and filled his mug with steaming coffee. Finally, as he recapped the jug, the phone was answered.

"Sweetman here. Did I wake you, Bubba?"

He and the man on the other end had had this conversation for more years than either cared to remember and the response was always the same on both ends.

"No. I was just screwin' my brains out."

Sweetman laughed as though it were the first time he'd heard the stale joke and then retorted, "Well I'm ready to do some screwin', myself."

"I ain't surprised," replied the man in Philadelphia. "Hasn't let up a bit. Suppose she's creakin' at the seams."

"Yeah. At this rate I `spect the river'll rise to meet us. I checked the weather and seems it'll be with us probably fer `nother twelve hours. Recommend holding it open longer'n usual so's we don't have to do it again tomorrow when the river's busy. You got any problems with that?"

"No. Nary a one. You're the best judge. You got the green light from here whenever you're ready."

Sweetman said good-night and hung up. Then, noting the time, he entered it into his log and stepped over to the control panel. It was exactly 1:35 when he flipped the row of red switches. Instantly, the tower began vibrating as the enormous cog wheels below cranked down the thick steel barriers atop the concrete wall allowing tons of water to escape over the Conowingo Dam spillway. In less than ten minutes the final leg of the rambling Susquehanna River would rise precipitously as a surge of water rushed along the remaining five miles of shoreline down towards the broad Chesapeake.

In the interim, Dankworth had moved to the rear of the building, where he kicked the door that he'd partially pried away from the frame earlier. Under the force of his boot it had yielded with a sharp splintering sound that echoed through the empty building. Not understanding any of it, Trish had remained huddled while trying to ignore the burning of her wounds. But there was little time for that, when moments later she heard a strange, menacing whooshing that rose in pitch until it blanked out the heavy rain. Seconds later the building trembled and her world erupted as the night was suddenly filled with the deafening roar of rotary engines. Before she understood what was happening the quadrangle was bathed in blinding light while a gale force wind whipped up every loose branch, board and shingle and tossed them, along with the rain and stones against the building and in through the open doorway she had entered only minutes earlier. With the light came earsplitting gunfire. Terrified, she curled into a tight ball and covered her head with her arms. In what seemed like a scene from hell, large caliber bullets were smashing into every building, tearing out plywood window covers and ripping apart the huge, heavy doors fronting the quad.

At that precise moment, Alfa and Bravo teams were dislodging the doors in the tunnels. With their guns leveled, the two men of Alfa ran down the hallway toward the mids while Bravo headed for the clock tower. There was only one guard left in the basement, the radioman, who foolishly stepped into the passageway. Before he got off a round, a spray of nine millimeters lifted him and flung his flailing body against the wall, leaving a gaping hole where his chest had been. In less than a minute Alfa had completed a room-to-room search of the basement before stopping at the door where they believed the mids to be. Wasting no time, the commando slid the bolt back then stopped at the sound of a hesitant, but insistent plea from the other side.

"Help us," Ingrid shouted while pressing her full weight against the door.

"U. S. Navy SEALs here," came the welcome response through the door.

"Don't! Don't open the door!" she screamed. "There's a bomb on this side!" Then she heard someone mutter, "Fuck!"

"Okay. Okay," the rescuer shouted back to her. "Stay cool." Then, turning to his teammate, who had now stationed himself at the head of the passageway, he called, "Get Timmy down here right away! We got a bomb."

Outside, under the Blackhawks' protective fire all twenty-eight SEALs had fast roped 120 feet into the quadrangle in three seconds and were scattering across the wide stretch of field in a blur of shadows. With bullets from Dankworth's men kicking at their feet, they fanned out to the five Tome school buildings while the helo crews disengaged the ropes to prevent them from fouling the rotor blades. Withholding their fire now that the SEALs were on the ground, the birds rose to 250 feet, where they kept their powerful searchlights on the buildings to inhibit the enemy's vision.

With the same clockwork precision as their Alfa teammates across the quad, the two Bravo commandos made it to the second floor with little resistance, where they could hear the steady crack of enemy gunfire in the clock tower above them.

"Bravo," Sampson shouted into his radio from behind a fifteen inch slab of broken concrete that had once been a border around the old athletic field. "You read me, Bravo?" He and two of his men were face down in the mud with rounds from the tower getting dangerously close.

"Bravo, aye."

"The tower's got us in their sights. Get your asses up there!"

"We're on our way, Skipper."

As Sampson ticked off the seconds one of the helos took a hit and he heard the tail rotor snap and the engine sputter. It was the one above him. Without enough air space to autorotate, the giant bird tumbled like a pinwheel. Fearing the damn thing would land on him, he was about to chance running through the fire storm when suddenly it jerked to the left and crashed fifty yards ahead, directly in front of the building where Dankworth was hiding.

The ground shuddered and Sampson saw the two gunners thrown clear of the wreckage. But before they could scramble for cover, Dankworth was in the doorway spraying them. They fell right away and he turned his weapon on the shattered cockpit with pinpoint accuracy, hitting both the pilot and co-pilot. In the next moment the fuel ignited, turning the crippled bird into a blazing hulk and Dankworth disappeared back inside.

With his line of sight obstructed by the wreckage, Sampson could do little more than watch the slaughter.

The time from Bravo's last transmission to when they finally reached the base of the tower was less than a minute. Spurred by the crack of gunfire directly above him, the snake eater crept up the spiral stairs to where he could see the feet of his enemies and tossed two flash bangs into the copper structure then dropped to the floor below. In the tight space the powerful concussion killed both men rather than stunning them. Seconds later, Sampson heard, "Bravo to Skipper, all clear."

While Bravo was working the tower problem, Timmy had raced through the tunnel in response to Alfa's call.

"Got a problem here, Timmy," the team leader said as he approached him. "From the way she describes it, sounds like the fuckers hung a bomb with a mercury switch on the back of the door." Then, anticipating the question, he said, "This is the only way in."

Timmy nodded. "You tell them not to move it?" he asked while studying the door frame and noting the air space at the base.

"Yep. But she'd already figured that out."

"Okay. Listen carefully," Timmy said to Ingrid, "Describe what you see."

"A leather knapsack, hung on a hook. The flap is loose. That's where the wire was before he pulled it out," she said in a clear, crisp voice.

Timmy was reassured by her steady tone and he said, "Without moving the bag, lift the flap and look inside, please. Tell me what you see."

While she did as she was told, Timmy turned to his companion and asked, "How much of this place have you guys secured?" The sound of gunfire continued unabated outside.

"Only this level. Larry's down there, watching the stairs," he nodded toward the end of the long hallway. "Gold should be clearing upstairs soon...," As he spoke the ground shook from the downed helo and Timmy said, "Shit. Doesn't sound good."

"Back up Larry," he instructed the man. "I'll work this problem."

"Looks like sticks of dynamite connected to some kind of switch," Ingrid called back.

"Do you see two wires leading to the switch?"

There was a pause followed by, "Yes. One black, the other red. Must be the circuit," she offered.

Good for you, Timmy thought to himself. "Can you reach them?" he asked.

"Yes. They're right on top. Want me to disconnect them," she said.

Timmy shook his head at her lack of fear. "Hold on. One step at a time." He withdrew a wire cutter from his pocket and slid it beneath the door. "Use this. Be sure, afterwards, they aren't touching."

The cutters were withdrawn and Timmy stepped aside, keeping his back against the concrete wall while beads of sweat formed on his blackened face.

"Done!" Her shout was triumphant.

"Step away from the door," he directed before cautiously pushing it open.

Minutes later, with the aid of a lock cutter, he had freed the mids and was herding them into the hallway.

"Ready to move `em to the tunnel," he shouted down the hall to his teammates. "All clear?"

"Roger," the one called, Larry shouted.

"Okay," Timmy said as he directed them single file down the hall. "Hustle."

Ingrid was the last out and rather than following the others, she turned and ran in the opposite direction.

"What the hell!" Timmy shouted, as he watched her snatch the mercenary's gun from his dead grip.

"Don't worry," she said, returning to his side. "I'm a marksman." Then, patting the gun with her injured hand, she said, "Just in case I see one of them."

"Well, don't shoot any SEALs," he said, slapping her on the back as they hurried to catch the others.

Outside, the battle continued but with less intensity now that the tower had been taken. Using night vision scopes, Bravo divided the compound into quadrants and was systematically suppressing the gunfire from the roofs of the other buildings.

On the ground, Gold team moved in and occupied building one, while Blue, under Cort's command, fought their way through the two old dormitories at the north end of the quad. Uncertain what traps lay behind closed doors or around blind corners, each team moved cautiously with flash bangs and sporadic gun bursts marking their progress from floor to floor. As they secured each level they tossed the bodies from windows into the quad below.

The only building still unentered was the one in which Sampson had seen Dankworth. Gunfire from it had been sporadic and came from various windows, causing him to question the number of men inside. Moving deliberately, he and two SEALs approached from three sides. They maneuvered in the shadows to within twenty-five yards without drawing fire. Then, a burst from a side window caught the man to Sampson's left. His legs buckled and he fell forward into the mud. Moments later, from a second window at the opposite end of the building, another series of rounds struck the man to his right. Unwilling to retreat and unable to go forward, Sampson found himself trapped again, this time behind the smoldering helo.

"Looks like an old fashioned western shootout." The rain muffled the words but there was no mistaking it was Dankworth taunting him.

Refusing to be baited, Sampson edged around the rear of the bird but was stopped by a spray of bullets that struck the ground just inches from his foot.

"Sonofabitch has night goggles," he thought to himself.

"I'm gonna kill you, you lousy cocksucker!" Dankworth shouted down on him before ripping apart the damaged tail section above Sampson's head with another volley.

"Blue, do you read me?" Sampson whispered into his radio.

"Loud and clear, Gold."

"I'm stuck behind the downed hawk. Do you have line of sight?"

Another spray hit the helo before the response came, driving him into the mud.

"I thought this would be harder, asshole. How `bout shooting back?" Dankworth called from a corner window on the first floor.

"He's on the first floor, right hand side. Hit him with the RAW," Sampson said.

"Can do. You better dig in."

"Don't worry about me. Just hit the fucker!" he said as he moved to avoid the shrapnel.

Cort turned to the man beside him with the Rifle Assault Weapon. They were on the second floor of a building across the quad, approximately 200 feet from Sampson.

"You heard the boss," he said.

The SEAL raised his M-16 rifle, sighted the window through his scope and fired. Sampson had prepared himself by crouching behind the helo. The man's aim was perfect and the two pound, rocket-assisted charge took out a chunk of the building, sending debris in a wide arc. Before it hit the ground Sampson was up and running at an angle toward the blown out window. Reaching it, he dove in, rolled and lay with his machine gun pointed away from the jagged hole.

The old dining hall was empty and, except for bits of crumbling plaster and the rain, quite still. Taking no chances, he remained fixed in the center of the room straining to detect any motion or sound above the wild beating in his chest. After a moment his attention was drawn to the broken door flapping in the wind at the rear of the building. Edging to the wall, he crept forward with his finger planted firmly against the trigger. Fifteen feet away he saw the plywood cover held in place by the top hinge. He waited a moment then darted for it. As he pushed it aside he recognized the sticky residue of wet blood and thought, Good. They got the bastard.

He knew from his recon and the photos that the rear of the building sat about thirty feet back from the perimeter fence. Moving cautiously, he approached the chain link fence and found where it had been cut away in the shape of an inverted V, with both edges curled up from the bottom. He stepped through and made his way to the ledge of the palisade. From there it was a two hundred foot drop to the town and the old port. If Dankworth had come this way, there had to be a way down. Sure enough, he found it at the tree line; a steep, narrow path that zigzagged down the face of the cliff and emerged at street level, across from the rail tracks. Loose rocks and streams of cascading water slowed his descent. Twice he lost his footing and nearly fell off. He was about thirty feet above street level when he spotted Dankworth moving toward the river. Despite the poor visibility there was no mistaking his huge bulk. Like a good SEAL, he was drawing Sampson to the water. But, he wasn't alone. To his surprise, the other person looked to be a woman but the near-horizontal rain prevented him from seeing her clearly, and he assumed Dankworth had taken one of the mids hostage. "It won't help you, you bastard," he cursed as he scrambled down the slope. "You're dead."

Reaching the base of the cliff, he dropped into a patch of weeds and studied the terrain before moving to the street.

Once again, Dankworth was waiting for him and when he emerged, he fired twice, but not at him. Wanting to kill Sampson up close, *mano a mano*, he'd aimed high so that the rounds cut into the ridge above the SEAL. It was his way of telling Sampson he knew he was there. Sampson hit the ground and rolled and when he looked up again Dankworth and the woman had reached the pier.

Dankworth was surprised to find the river flowing with such velocity and much higher than his charts had indicated. A nuisance, he thought, but not a deterrence to his planned showdown.

Meanwhile, Sampson watched from across the street with curious fascination. He could hear the flooding river and wondered what Dankworth had in mind. Searching the shoreline, he expected to see a small craft pre-positioned there as a contingency, but there was none. He was also troubled by the woman. And while there was something familiar about her, he couldn't linger on it. It was critical that he stay focused on closing the distance between him and Bull and protecting himself in the process. Squatting below the track bed, he darted across the street and in doing so temporarily lost sight of Dankworth.

But Dankworth had seen him coming and when Sampson scrambled up the incline he fired off several rounds. This time, he was aiming to hit and one bullet ripped into Sampson's left thigh. The force sent him spinning between two large wooden spools, the type used to hold telephone wire. He landed hard and without his machine gun.

"Gotcha!" Dankworth sang out with an intoxicated laugh.

They were close enough now that neither the rain nor the surging river muffled his resonant voice. Sampson grimaced not at the wound but at the taunting. He knew his adversary well. In a sense, they were alike. Both had a zest for combat and found passion in warfare. Unfortunately, he thought sourly, Dankworth took it to extremes.

Before he could advance, three more rounds splintered the wheel above his head forcing him down behind the spool. Grabbing his leg, he probed the wound and found the bullet had torn the flesh but missed his bone and muscle. He was bleeding but not profusely. Rolling over, he pulled out his Beretta, cocked it, and fired to the left of the woman, who Bull had now backed up against the nearest piling. Shooting while the two of them were together was chancy. Had she moved he might have killed her. But she was staying perfectly still. His aim was off and it gave Dankworth a chance to sprint to the end of the pier leaving the woman behind. Wisely, she remained still, keeping out of the line of fire.

Again, he couldn't understand why Bull was deliberately putting himself in a corner and leaving his cover behind. But it didn't matter, whatever the reason, he'd pursue him. There was a third spool twenty feet ahead. Favoring his injured leg, he darted for it and dove the last several feet as Dankworth's rounds shot up the stones behind him. He was now less than fifteen feet from the woman and what he saw sickened and angered him. It was Trish and Dankworth had impaled her through the throat to the piling with his knife. She looked pitiful. In addition to the clean knife wound there were large, ugly bruises on her face and chest.

"A little present for you, Dukie boy. Like it?" he shouted from behind the last piling about thirty feet beyond. "That's what I'm going to do to you, you worthless sonofabitch."

Outraged, Sampson placed his shoulder against the heavy wooden spool and, digging into the soft gravel, pushed hard. But the large wheels refused to move. Meanwhile, Dankworth understood what he was doing and he emptied his clip in a fusillade, sending splinters flying above the SEAL's head. Undaunted, Sampson took a deep breath, dug in and, ignoring his wound and the blood that had oozed into his boot, leaned into the wheel. This time it moved, slowly at first, then with enough momentum to enable him to angle it down the track bed and onto the pier. As he directed the spool past Trish's limp body, the pier lurched and swayed from the added burden. The wheels were turning faster now and breaking up chunks of rotting wood that were quickly swept away by the swirling river that had risen to within inches of the planks beneath his feet.

With nothing but the black river behind him, Dankworth stood his ground and reloaded. The obscenities he hurled at Sampson penetrated the storm and the rolling thunder of the advancing spool. Consumed with their own personal fury, neither man heard nor noticed the cracking and splitting boards.

With the spool moving freely, Sampson gave his portable fortress a final shove and, disregarding the water spraying up between the planks, he knelt and steadied his aim until Dankworth came into view.

For a moment both men were frozen in time. Then, glimpsing Dankworth through the rain, he raised his gun and fired twice and then twice again. On the last shot the pier shuddered violently then crumbled, pitching the two rivals into the turbulence below.

In an instant everything was swept away, leaving behind only a single, gruesome clue that a pier had once been there - the lone piling by the shore from which Trish now dangled like a limp doll.

D-Day

Chapter Twenty-Two

Lucerne's car pulled away from the Pentagon at 9:15 and onto the parkway. He was on his way to the White House after a long, stressful night. And though exhausted, it was the first time he wasn't haunted by the debilitating fear that he'd worked so hard to suppress since the kidnapping.

When word had reached him that the mids were safe, he immediately called his wife and then left for Bethesda Naval Hospital while the vice president notified Pickens and the Bennetts. He arrived at the emergency room shortly after three, twenty minutes before the first medivac helo came in with the injured SEALs. With the hospital's commanding officer at his side, the four-star general expressed his gratitude and that of the president's to the medical staff, who had been on a twelve hour standby without knowing why. Until then, for security reasons, only the commanding officer had been briefed. As Lucerne looked around the emergency room at the staff he was reminded of similar scenes he'd witnessed in Vietnam, in which grim-faced medics gathered expectantly at triage stations, listening attentively to incoming helo transmissions, as they were doing now.

Ingrid and her classmates were on the second helo. And when she darted into his arms, Lucerne knew immediately from the fire in her eyes that she'd come through the ordeal in good shape. And though they had only a few minutes together before she was taken away to begin the lengthy medical evaluation, it was enough to dispel his fears.

Now, on his way across the Potomac, he chuckled to himself, aware it was the first time he'd found any humor during the past ten days. He was staring at the muddy river and thinking of when Ingrid had kissed him on the cheek as she climbed atop the gurney to be wheeled into the examining room and then handed him the gun she'd tucked in her waistband.

"Here. Keep an eye on this for me, please," she had said. Then, with a smile and a wink, she added, "Be careful. There's a round in the chamber."

Lucerne found Hemmings just inside the entrance to the White House. He had been waiting there out of the rain to greet his friend before joining the others inside.

"How is she, John?" he asked, grabbing Lucerne's hand as he spoke.

"She's going to be fine, Ray. I've just talked with the doctors and they're very upbeat about her condition." His relaxed expression said it all. "Miriam's there with her now. There's no reason why she can't come home tonight." Then, his expression changed and he said, "Sorry to report that won't be the case for one of her classmates. Poor child underwent a brutal assault." He shook his head. "Her body will heal, but at this point they can't be certain about her mind. A real tragedy," he said with obvious distress.

"What a pity," Hemmings said, as they walked to the NSC meeting room.

In the conference room the vice president came over and told Lucerne, "The president has asked that I convey to you and Miriam his sincerest best wishes upon the safe return of your daughter."

"Thank you," Lucerne said with a nod. "I'll be sure to tell her."

While the ordeal with the mids was over, there were still other matters that needed the NSC's attention. And they moved quickly to them.

"What casualties did we suffer?" Mack asked Lucerne as they settled into their seats.

"We lost seven. Four Army. Two SEALs and one civilian. Additionally, there are three wounded. All SEALs. And one MIA, also a SEAL," he said.

"Civilian? MIA?" Mack said.

Lucerne told them about Trish Mathews and how Sampson's rifle had been found not far from her body and the battered pier. "The conjecture among the SEALs who had seen him enter the building where Dankworth was hiding," he explained, "is that he pursued him and the newswoman to the river. They think both men were washed away when the pier collapsed." His mood was somber.

"We've had Coast Guard boats and helos searching since first light," he continued, "but we haven't had any success in locating either man. The SEALs are conducting their own extensive search along both shorelines. We'll have a clearer idea, and God willing, better news by noon."

"And the terrorists?" Diamond asked.

"With the exception of Dankworth, we believe we have all twenty-two accounted for. All dead. Twenty-one by the SEALs and one by the FBI agents guarding the perimeter."

"How'd our SEALs let one slip through the net?" Hemmings' comment released the tension briefly and they laughed.

"Don't know yet. But, I'm sure they'll give it their close attention during their hot wash up," Lucerne replied.

"Would've been interesting if they had captured that one," Mack said.

"The FBI tried, but he didn't want it that way. They caught him after he'd slipped through the fence near the reservoir. When they ordered him to drop his weapons and put his hands up, he shouted something in German then began firing at them. They had no choice."

With not much more to report, they moved on to the Iranian problem with Harrison, from State, briefing them on his progress.

"Everything's in place," he began. "Our allies have been notified and the demarche and ultimatum will be delivered at noon...,"

* * *

While the U. S. ambassador to the United Nations was delivering both documents to his Iranian counterpart, two SEALs were beaching their small boat on the rugged shoreline of Garrett Island, located two miles down river from Port Deposit. Thirty-five minutes after landing they found Sampson on the far side, wedged between two large boulders, five feet above the normal water line. He'd lost a considerable amount of blood but he was very much alive as evidenced by his comment.

"What the hell took you so long?" he asked when they reached him.

The search for Dankworth continued for three days, extending beyond the Susquehanna and into the broader coastal waters of the northern Chesapeake, all without positive results.

* * *

At 10:00 pm, EST (5:00 am, Saudi time), the National Security Agency monitoring communications in the gulf picked up indications of Tehran's intent to disregard the U. S. ultimatum. With Irani gunboats moving toward the Saudi coastline Vice President Mack, in session with the NSC, authorized the Kitty Hawk Task Force Commander to sink Iran's two Russian Kilo submarines and ordered Commander Cherico to launch conventional Tomahawk missiles from the Annapolis against Iran's naval command post, in Bandar Abbas. Further, he instructed that their UN ambassador be notified immediately that long range B-52 bombers flying from Diego Garcia, in the Indian Ocean, were moving toward Iran with the intent of attacking key infrastructures, including national energy sources and most specifically, Iran's partially constructed 300-megawatt nuclear power plant in Bushehr, if there wasn't an immediate pullback of all deployed forces.

Epilogue

President Leslie Pickens recovered soon after the Iranian problem was resolved. But then, several weeks later, he suffered severe mood disturbances, compounded by manic episodic swings which were manifested by irritability, hyperactivity, rapid speech, flights of ideas and temper tantrums. At his physician's urging, he was admitted to Bethesda and subsequently diagnosed as having Bipolar Disorder. The team of doctors examining him attributed his condition to trauma experienced as a child in an alcoholic family and the stress brought on during the preceding month. While confident that he would recover, they emphasized continued medication and the need for a total abstinence from stress. With some gentle persuasion from his wife, the vice president and Senator Bennett, Pickens agreed to resign and return to his southern roots and the family's agricultural business. Mrs. Pickens, however, chose to remain in Washington, where she serves on several boards and commissions.

Vice President Mack took the oath of presidency and subsequently set about reversing many of his predecessor's policies, beginning with his program of downsizing the armed forces.

Ironically, the failed attempt to overtake Saudi Arabia strengthened Iran's military leaders' position within their government while eroding the once-powerful moderate Islamic clerics. With the aid of Russian technology, construction of the nuclear power plant continues despite concerns among western nations that it would ultimately enable Iran to produce weapons-grade plutonium as early as 2001. Undeterred, Iran recently entered into negotiations with North Korea to purchase three of its Soviet-designed, Romeo-class diesel submarines, each capable of firing 14 torpedoes or launching 28 mines. Nor did Iran's setback alter the vitriol it continues to hurl at its centuries-old neighbor. The Persians have accused Baghdad of aggressive border incursions while demanding that Iraq cease arming Iran's exiled, People's Mojahedin army.

For their part, the Saudi Royal Family persists in disregarding Iran's criticism concerning their irresponsible stewardship of the holy land. Instead, the king continues his extravagant lifestyle and wasteful spending despite falling oil prices and the country's annual 3.5 percent population growth, which world economists predict is a sure formula for economic collapse.

Midshipman Bennett informed Admiral Harding he no longer possessed the drive and the motivation to fulfill the demanding role of a naval officer. With the admiral's blessings, he will complete his final semester and accept a medical discharge upon graduating. His father, Senator Bennett, supported his son's decision while encouraging him to pursue a law degree as a prerequisite to embarking on a political career.

Midshipman Lucerne briefly considered prodding the Navy to allow her to enter SEAL training, but opted instead for a commission in the Marine Corps and flight training.

After recuperating, Commander Sampson returned to his unit. Though results of the Navy's promotion boards are never revealed prior to approval by the president, smart money has it that even though he isn't eligible for promotion for two more years, his name will be among the newly selected captains. When the list is published, Sampson can expect a transfer to the Joint Chiefs of Staff, where he'll serve as Joint Services Special Forces Coordinator as well as Director Mission Activities in the office of the Assistant Secretary of Defense for Special Operations and Low Intensity Conflict, a position that will surely lead to promotion to flag rank.

To date, Dankworth's body has not surfaced nor has he been sighted alive anywhere. Nevertheless, his vital statistics, including his aliases, continue to be carried in the FBI's data bank of most wanted criminals.

Midshipmen First Class Valerius and Zablocki were buried with full honors at the Naval Academy. Visitors to the school will find their names on the list of alumni who died in the service of their country. An asterisk beside their names, indicates they died in hostile action while midshipmen. The modest looking, but lengthy roster is proudly displayed along the center wall of the Hall of Heroes, in Bancroft Hall.

To date, the Naval Academy remains open to the public but access to classroom buildings is now restricted to midshipmen and faculty. As acts of terrorism become more prevalent within the United States it can be assumed that security will become tighter, still. We pray it does before another such incident.

the end

About the Author

George Vercessi is a retired U.S. Navy captain who developed and co-produced "The Silver Strand," an MGM film aired on ShowTime. He has also written several novels and numerous short stories.

He is a member of the Authors Guild, the Virginia Writers Club and the Washington Independent Writers.